Other Books by Elizabeth Hardwick

The Ghostly Lover
The Simple Truth
A View of My Own
Selected Letters of William James

Seduction and Betrayal

Seduction *AND* Betrayal

WOMEN AND LITERATURE

Elizabeth Hardwick

 Random House / New York

Grateful acknowledgment is made to the following for permission to reprint previously published material:

Farrar, Straus & Giroux, Inc., and Chatto & Windus Ltd.: For seven lines from "The Fish," from *The Complete Poems of Elizabeth Bishop.* Copyright 1940, © 1969 by Elizabeth Bishop.

Harper & Row Publishers, Inc., and Miss Olwyn Hughes: For specified excerpts from "Daddy," "Lady Lazarus," "Lesbos," "Edge," "Cut," "Contusion," "Death & Co.," from *Ariel*, by Sylvia Plath. Copyright © 1965 by Ted Hughes. Specified excerpt from "Last Words," from *Crossing the Water*, by Sylvia Plath. Copyright © 1971 by Ted Hughes. Specified excerpts from "For a Fatherless Son" and "Apprehensions," from *Winter Trees*, by Sylvia Plath. Copyright © 1972 by Ted Hughes.

Harper & Row Publishers, Inc., and Faber and Faber Ltd.: For two lines from *Wodwo*, by Ted Hughes. Copyright © 1967 by Ted Hughes.

Harper & Row Publishers, Inc., and The Bodley Head: For specified excerpts from *Zelda*, by Nancy Milford. Copyright © 1970 by Nancy Winston Milford.

Macmillan Publishing Co., Inc., and Faber and Faber Ltd.: For nine lines from "Smooth Gnarled Crape Myrtle," from *The Complete Poems of Marianne Moore.* Copyright 1941 and renewed 1969 by Marianne Moore.

Indiana University Press and Faber and Faber Ltd.: For two lines by Anne Sexton from *The Art of Sylvia Plath*, edited by Charles Newman (1970).

Library of Congress Cataloging in Publication Data

Lowell, Elizabeth Hardwick
  Seduction and betrayal; women and literature.

  1. Women authors.   2.   Women in literature.
I. Title.
PN471.H3   809'.933'52   73–3982
ISBN 0–394–49069–X

Manufactured in the United States of America
98765432
First Edition

These essays have been, since their publication in *The New York Review of Books,* altered in some cases, expanded in others. "Seduction and Betrayal" was read at Vassar College in 1972; "The Brontës" and the essays on Dorothy Wordsworth and Jane Carlyle were part of three lectures given for the Christian Gauss Seminar in Criticism at Princeton University. I wish to express my gratitude to Robert Silvers for the most fundamental and varied help, and to Devie Meade and Professor Susan Turner for the many things I have learned from our long conversations about literature and history.

To my friend Barbara Epstein, with love

Contents

THE BRONTËS

THE CAREERS of the three Brontë sisters—Anne, Charlotte, and Emily—conferred a sort of perpetuity upon the whole family. The father's eccentricities, once brought under scrutiny by the fame of the daughters, proved to be rich enough in detail to provide a good store of anecdote. There is, as with all of the family, always some question about what was truth and what fancy.

The Reverend Brontë was a failed writer. He had published *Cottage Poems* and *The Rural Minstrel,* and he certainly had the sedentary habits and wide range of peculiarities that might have assisted a literary career, but perhaps the Reverend was not able to take in enough from the outside to nourish his art. He carried a pistol around with him and sometimes when he was angry found relief by shooting through the open door. It was rumored that he cut up one of his wife's silk dresses out of regard for his strict standards of simplicity and seriousness. For his own part the Reverend Brontë disowned claims to flamboyance and said: "I do not deny that I am somewhat eccentric. . . . Only don't set me on in my fury to burning hearthrugs, sawing the backs off chairs and tearing my wife's silk gowns."

There were five daughters and one son in the Brontë family, and the father unluckily placed his hopes in his son,

Branwell. It is only by accident that we know about people like Branwell who seemed destined for the arts, unable to work at anything else, and yet have not the talent, the tenacity, or the discipline to make any kind of sustained creative effort. With great hopes and at bitter financial sacrifice, Branwell was sent up to London to study painting at the Academy Schools. The experience was wretched for him and he seemed to have sensed his lack of preparation, his uncertain dedication, his faltering will. He never went to the school, did not present his letters of introduction, and spent his money in taverns drinking gin. It finally became necessary to return home in humiliation and to pretend that he had been robbed.

One story has poor Branwell visiting the National Gallery and, in the presence of the great paintings there, despairing of his own talents. This is hard to credit, since the example of the great is seldom a deterrent to the mediocre. In any case, nothing leads us to think Branwell lacked vanity or expansive ideas of his own importance. Also, the deterrent of Branwell's own nature made any further impediments unnecessary. His nature was hysterical, addictive, self-indulgent. Very early he fell under the spell of alcohol and opium; his ravings and miseries destroyed the family peace, absorbed their energies, and depressed their spirits. He had to be talked to, watched over, soothed, and protected—and nothing really availed. Branwell destroyed his life with drugs and drink, and died of a bronchial infection at the age of thirty-one.

Perhaps the true legacy Branwell left the world is to be found in the extraordinary violence of feeling, the elaborate language of bitterness and frustration in *Wuthering Heights.* It is not unreasonable to see the origin of some of Heathcliff's raging disappointment and disgust in Branwell's own excited sense of injury and betrayal. Emily Brontë took toward her

brother an attitude of stoical pity and protectiveness. Charlotte was, on the other hand, in despair at his deterioration,
troubled by his weaknesses, and condemning of the pain he
brought to the household. It is significant that Charlotte
insisted Branwell did not know of the publication of his
sisters' poems, nor of the composition of *Wuthering Heights,
Jane Eyre,* and *Agnes Grey.* She wrote: "My unhappy
brother never knew what his sisters had done in literature—
he was not aware that they had ever published a line. We
could not tell him of our efforts for fear of causing him too
deep a pang of remorse for his own time misspent, and talents
misapplied."

Still, in spite of every failure and vice, Branwell always
interested people. The news of his promise and default
seemed to have spread around quite early. Matthew Arnold
included him in his poem "Haworth Churchyard," written
in 1855, the year of Charlotte Brontë's death and two years
before Mrs. Gaskell's biography. About Branwell, Arnold
wrote:

> O boy, if here thou sleep'st, sleep well:
> On thee too did the Muse
> Bright in thy cradle smile;
> But some dark shadow came
> (I know not what) and interposed.

The emergence of the Brontë sisters is altogether a lucky
circumstance and nothing is easier than to imagine all of
them dying unknown, their works lost. The father lived to
be eighty-four, but, of the children, Charlotte's survival to
thirty-nine seemed almost a miracle. Not even she, and certainly not the other two sisters, had the chance to do what
they might have. This is especially distressing in the case of
Emily. *Wuthering Heights* has a sustained brilliance and

originality we hardly know how to account for. It is on a different level of inspiration from her poetry; the grandeur and complication of it always remind one of the leap she might have taken had she lived.

They are an odd group, the Brontës, beaten down by a steady experience of the catastrophic. The success of *Jane Eyre,* the fame that came to Charlotte, were fiercely, doggedly earned. She had struggled for independence not as an exhilaration dreamed of but as a necessity, a sort of grocery to sustain the everyday body and soul. Literary work and the presence of each other were the consolations at Haworth parsonage. There was certainly a family closeness because of the dangers they had passed through in the deaths of their mother and two older sisters. Haworth was a retreat; but part of its hold upon them was a kind of negative benevolence: it was at least better to have the freedom and familiarity of the family than the oppression of the life society offered to penniless, intellectual girls.

A study of the Brontë lives leaves one with a disorienting sense of the unexpected and the paradoxical in their existence. In them are combined simplicities and exaggerations, isolation and an attraction to scandalous situations. They are very serious, wounded, longing women, conscious of all the romance of literature and of their own fragility and suffering. They were serious about the threatening character of real life. Romance and deprivation go hand in hand in their novels. Quiet and repressed the sisters may have been, but their readers were immediately aware of a disturbing undercurrent of intense sexual fantasy. Loneliness and melancholy seemed to alternate in their feelings with an unusual energy and ambition.

In the novels of Charlotte and Anne there is a firm grasp of social pressures and forces; they understand from their own experience that opportunities for independence were likely to be crushing in other ways to the essential spirit and the sense of self. In *Wuthering Heights* the characters are struggling with an inner tyranny, a psychic trap more terrible than the cruelty of society. The characters feed upon themselves and each other. They are set apart, without relation to anything beyond. The young people of the two families have only the trap of each other and the tyranny of the past. The sweep of existence is stripped of the environmental and the particular. In the same manner, the sense of place, the moors, the houses, are spiritual locations. There is a scarcity of scene painting, even though the sense of place is very strong, as a cell or a dungeon would be. The moors provide the isolation, the loneliness, and the removal that are essential to the story. So even nature is negative, serving to relieve the characters of the expectations of a usual society, of interdependence. It is a created, imagined world, as removed from the governess-novels of the other sisters as any world could be.

Catherine, in *Wuthering Heights,* is nihilistic, self-indulgent, bored, restless, nostalgic for childhood, unmanageable. She has the charm of a wayward, schizophrenic girl, but she has little to give, since she is self-absorbed, haughty, destructive. What is interesting and contemporary for us is that Emily Brontë should have given Catherine the center of the stage, to share it along with the rough, brutal Heathcliff. In a novel by Charlotte or Anne, Cathy would be a shallow beauty, analyzed and despaired of by a reasonable, clever and deprived heroine. She would be fit only for the subplot. There is also an unromantic driven egotism in the characters, a lack of moral longings, odd in the work of a daughter of a clergyman.

Emily Brontë's poetry is constricted by its hymn-tune rhythms and a rather narrow and provincial idea of the way to use her own peculiar visions. The novel form released in her a new and explosive spirit. The demands of the form, the setting, the multiplication of incidents, the need to surround the Byronic principals, Cathy and Heathcliff, with the prosaic—the dogs, the husbands, the family servants, sisters, houses—the elements of fact lift up the dreamlike, compulsive figures, give them life. The plot of *Wuthering Heights* is immensely complicated and yet there is the most felicitous union of author and subject. There is nothing quite like this novel with its rage and ragings, its discontent and angry restlessness.

Wuthering Heights is a virgin's story. The peculiarity of it lies in the harshness of the characters. Cathy is as hard, careless, and destructive as Heathcliff. She too has a sadistic nature. The love the two feel for each other is a longing for an impossible completion. Consolations do not appear; nothing in the domestic or even in the sexual life seems to the point in this book. Emily Brontë appears in every way indifferent to the need for love and companionship that tortured the lives of her sisters. We do not, in her biography, even look for a lover as we do with Emily Dickinson because it is impossible to join her with a man, with a secret, aching passion for a young curate or a schoolmaster. There is a spare, inviolate center, a harder resignation amounting finally to withdrawal.

The Brontë sisters had the concentration and energy that marked the great nineteenth-century literary careers. When *The Professor* was going the rounds of publishers, Charlotte was finishing *Jane Eyre.* The publication of the *Poems by Currer, Ellis and Acton Bell* was just barely a publication. A year later only two copies had been sold and the book received merely a few scattered, unimportant notices. Still, it was an emergence, an event, an excitement. Emily had at first resisted publication and was so guarded about the failure of the book that we cannot judge her true feelings. No discouragement prevented the sisters from starting to work, each one, on a novel. The practical side of publication, the proofs, the letters to editors, the seriousness of public authorship were an immensely significant break in the isolation and uncertainty of their lives.

The Brontës had always had a sense of performance, of home performance in their Angria and Gondal plots and characters. And some of them quite early felt their gifts could reasonably claim the attention of the world. Branwell wrote high-handed letters to the editor of *Blackwood's Magazine* saying, "Do you think your magazine so perfect that no additions to its power would be either possible or desirable?" He sent off a note to Wordsworth suggesting, "Surely, in this day when there is not a writing poet worth a sixpence, the field must be open, if a better man can step forward." Wordsworth noted the mixture of "gross flattery" and "plenty of abuse" and did not reply.

Charlotte posted a few poems to Southey. He was not discourteous but delivered the opinion, "Literature cannot be the business of a woman's life, and it ought not to be. The more she is engaged in her proper duties, the less leisure will she have for it, even as an accomplishment and a recreation."

Absolute need drove the Brontë sisters. They were poor, completely dependent upon their father's continuation in his post, and without hopes of anything were he to die. They did receive a small legacy upon the death of Aunt Branwell and they looked upon the income with awe and intense gratitude. But it was not in any sense a living. The sisters were not beautiful, yet their appearance can hardly be thought a gross liability. Their natures, the scars of the deaths of their mother and sisters, their intellectuality, and their poverty were the obstacles to marriage.

There was also perhaps some disappointment in their father and brother that weighed on their spirits. Branwell's imperfections were large and memorable; the father's were less palpable. He was not a rock—at least not of the right kind. When Charlotte finally married his curate he refused to perform the ceremony and indeed gave up altogether the duty of marrying persons. The Brontë household was in fact a household of women, women living and dead. The sense of being on their own came very early. Each sister felt the weight of responsibility in an acute and thorough way.

The worries that afflicted genteel, impoverished women in the nineteenth century can scarcely be exaggerated. They were cut off from the natural community of the peasant classes. The world of Tess of the D'Urbervilles, for all its sorrow and injustice, is more open and warm and fresh than the cramped, anxious, fireside-sewing days of the respectable. Chaperones, fatuous rules of deportment and occupation drained the energy of intelligent, needy women. Worst of all was society's contempt for the prodigious efforts they made to survive. Their condition was dishonorable, but no approval attached to their efforts to cope with it. The humiliations endured in the work of survival are a great part of the actual material in the fiction of Charlotte and Anne Brontë.

It seems likely that there was a steady downward plunge by alliances with the poorer classes on the part of the desperate daughters of impecunious gentlefolk. And some resolved to move upward, like Becky Sharp, the daughter of a dissolute painter and an opera-singer mother. Becky Sharp had "the dismal precocity of poverty" and the heedless shrewdness of the bohemian world. She spoke of herself as never having been a girl: ". . . she had been a woman since she was eight years old." Becky Sharp is the perfect contrast to Jane Eyre and Lucy Snowe, the heroine of Charlotte Brontë's *Villette,* two girls with an almost extinguishing sense of determination and accountability. In the Brontë sisters there is a distinctly high tone and low spirit; they retained something of the Methodism of their mother and of the aunt who raised them. Even Branwell, with his flaming indulgences, is a sort of prototypical parson's son who exchanged every prohibition for a license.

Charlotte Brontë wrote: "None but those who had been in a position of a governess could ever realize the dark side of respectable human nature; under no great temptation to crime, but daily giving way to selfishness and ill-temper, till its conduct toward those dependent on it sometimes amounts to a tyranny of which one would rather be the victim than the inflicter." To be a lady's companion was even worse for a young woman; the caprice and idleness of the old fell down like a shroud upon the young.

Schools had always been traumatic and even murderous for the Brontë children. The two older daughters, Maria and Elizabeth, were sent to the Clergy Daughters' School, an institution especially endowed for girls like themselves who could expect to have to make their own way. It was sponsored by such well-known people of the day as Wilberforce and Hannah More. But the school was, nevertheless, a cruel place—cold, with inadequate, dirty food, and overworked, tyrannical teachers. The children took long freezing walks to church and sat in their cold, damp clothes all day. There was tuberculosis throughout the school, and the condition led to the death of Maria when she was twelve and Elizabeth when she was eleven. Emily and Charlotte were only six and a half and eight years old when they joined their older sisters at the school. They watched with horror and the deepest resentment as the older girls fell ill and were sent home to die.

The mother of the Brontës had died of cancer after bearing six children in seven years. All of these griefs and losses formed the character of the survivors: the religious earnestness of Anne; the withdrawn, peculiar nature of Emily; the stoical determination of Charlotte.

For the sisters, and even for Branwell after his failure as a painter, life seemed to offer nothing except the position of governess or tutor in a private family. This was a hard destiny. The children exploit and torment; the parents exploit and ignore. The social and family position of a governess was ambiguous and led to painful feelings of resentment, envy, or bitter acceptance. The young women who went to work in the houses of the well-to-do were clever and unprotected; one quality seemed to vex their charges and employers as much as the other.

The teacher-governess in fiction is likely, because of the intimate family setting in which she is living her lonely life, to fall into an almost hysterical, repressed eroticism. Henry James noticed the tendency of the governess to be "easily carried away." Both Jane Eyre and Lucy Snowe are superior, gifted girls, very much like Charlotte Brontë herself. They are bookish, forthright, skeptical, inclined to moralizing and to making wearisome, patient efforts to maintain self-esteem and independence. They are defenseless, cast adrift, and yet of an obviously fine quality that shows itself in a tart talent for down-putting retorts. Under the correcting surface they are deeply romantic, full of dreams, and visited by nightmares. They feel a pressing, hurting need for love and yet they work hard to build up resignation to the likelihood that they will have to live bereft of the affections so much wanted. Need and sublimation play back and forth like a wavering light over their troubled consciousness. By these pains they grew into sharp observers, ever anxious to control and manage a threatening despair.

From being a lowly governess in a private house one could hope to rise to the position of a teacher in a boarding school. And beyond that there was the wish to have a school of one's own—that was the hope of the Brontës as they faced their lack of money and the scarcity of possible husbands. Emily hated everything to do with women's education as she knew it in her own day and looked upon her home with its freedom and familiarity as an escape from school. Even for Charlotte, the idea of her own school was a goal but it was not her heart's desire. Instead it was a heavy charge to be thought of as propitious only by comparison with other possibilities.

Governesses were expected to give a shallow training to the young but were not ordinarily allowed the authority or respect that would make the training possible. In Anne Brontë's novel, *Agnes Grey,* the young pupils are so cruel and selfish the book was thought to be an exaggeration. In almost the first meeting with her charges the governess is taken to see a trap set for birds. When she remonstrates with a young pupil about this cruelty he is indifferent; she calls upon the authority of the parents and the boy says:

"Papa knows how I treat them [the birds] and he never blames me for it; he says it is just what *he* used to do when *he* was a boy. Last summer he gave me a nest full of young sparrows, and he saw me pulling off their legs and heads and never said anything; except that they were nasty things and I must not let them spoil my trousers. . . ."

Writing was an escape from this kind of servitude. In addition to their unusual gifts, the perils of their future created in the sisters a remarkable professionalism. The romantic aspects of their achieving anything at all have been inordinately insisted upon and the practical, industrious, ambitious cast of mind too little stressed. Necessity, dependence, discipline drove them hard; being a writer was a way of living, surviving, literally keeping alive. They worked to get their books published; they worried about contracts, knew the chagrins and misunderstandings of authorship. Emily was disappointed in the inane reception of *Wuthering*

Heights; Charlotte's first novel, *The Professor,* was turned down everywhere. (In fact, the crossed-out publishers' addresses on the manuscript showed her perseverance even if they were somewhat dampening to the receiver.)

In addition to the professionalism of the sisters, there was an unexpected inclination in the family to create scandal. Charlotte's books aroused a sense of unease in the reader and outrage in those people and institutions from real life she used in her stories. There was an oddly rebellious and erotic tone to the imaginings and plot developments of the little governesses.

Mrs. Gaskell's *Life of Charlotte Brontë* is one of the great English biographies. The two women had been friends, and some months after Charlotte's death in 1855 the Reverend Brontë asked Mrs. Gaskell to compose a memoir of his daughter. The book appeared in 1857 and the author rushed off to Rome for a holiday. Her celebration was soon disturbed by protest. Threats of legal action forced her to make alterations and deletions in the second edition and it was not until almost fifty years later that the original version could be read again.

Mrs. Gaskell's aim had been a true record of her friend's life with some underlining of Charlotte Brontë's "noble" character in order to counteract the accusations of "coarseness" and unruly emotionalism leveled at *Jane Eyre* and *Villette.* She suppressed certain findings—the most important was the real truth about Charlotte's experience in Belgium and her falling in love there with M. Heger. She rushed forward with certain other details, such as the truth about the Clergy Daughters' School and, more important, an account of Branwell's relation or infatuation with Mrs. Robinson.

Branwell had gone as a tutor to the Robinson family, where his sister Anne also held a post. He fell in love with

Mrs. Robinson, and was turned out of the house by the husband. There was nothing for Branwell to do except to return to Haworth in love and in disgrace, filled with impetuous longings and hysterical hopes. Mr. Robinson was somewhat older than his wife and soon died. When the news reached Branwell he allowed himself to believe he would now be sent for by his beloved. Instead Mrs. Robinson sent a courier with quite another message, one saying untruthfully that her husband had left her money in his will only on condition that she never see Branwell again. The news was given to Branwell at the Black Bull and here is Mrs. Gaskell's account of his feelings:

> More than an hour elapsed before sign or sound was heard; then those outside heard a noise like the bleating of a calf, and on opening the door, he [Branwell] was found in a kind of fit, succeeding the stupor of grief which he had fallen into on hearing that he was forbidden by his paramour ever to see her again, as if he did, she would forfeit her fortune. Let her live and flourish! He died, his pockets filled with her letters. . . . When I think of him, I change my cry to heaven. Let her live and repent!

Mrs. Gaskell's work is written with perfect sympathy, an experienced and inspired feeling for detail, and the purest assurance of style. Naturally it did not please in every respect. The father endured but made a list of deeds and traits wrongly attributed to him; Mr. Nicholls, Charlotte's husband, was pained to have Mrs. Gaskell reveal so fully Charlotte's early lack of enthusiasm for his proposal of marriage. Some have defended Emily from a rather bleak portrait by the author; servants gave a happier and healthier account of the parsonage diet than that found in the biography. Out of the withholdings on the one hand and the rash unfoldings on the other Mrs. Gaskell created some vexations for herself and left room for the efforts of future scholars.

Her biography is not only about Charlotte but contains the life of the entire family and certainly, appearing early as it did, gave a tremendous lift to the literary fortunes of the sisters and a boost to the "Brontë story." The book, in addition to being a marvelous work in itself, records the basic material: the town of Keighley, the Haworth parsonage, the anecdotes of home and school, the deaths, the letters, the poignant gifts and hard work of the sisters.

Winifred Gérin, a contemporary Brontë scholar, has spent seventeen years studying the life of the family and has lived for ten years in the village of Haworth. She has taken the family one by one: *Anne Brontë,* 1959; *Branwell Brontë,* 1961; *Charlotte Brontë: The Evolution of a Genius,* 1967, recently reissued; and in 1971 her final volume, *Emily Brontë.* Of these volumes the most interesting is the study of Charlotte Brontë. She lived longer than the others and her life was more filled with incident.

Mrs. Gérin does her work in a capable and thorough Brontë Society manner. She is an enthusiast, and rather exuberant and traditional in matters of style, and thus there is a good deal about "the beloved moors." She knows what is known at the moment and knows it so surely that she convinces us everything has been discovered, found, filed. In matters of interpretation she is not daring but tends more to an insistence on certain small points. In *Emily Brontë* a mystical, mysterious genius is sketched and colored, but no one and no amount of fact can give flesh to Emily Brontë's character. She is almost impossible to come to terms with, to visualize. At one moment—more violent in Mrs. Gaskell, toned down in Mrs. Gérin—Emily is brutally beating her dog about the eyes and face with her own fists in order to discourage him from his habit of slipping upstairs to take a nap on the clean counterpanes. At another time she is a reverent, pantheistic brooder.

A good deal is made in this book of the emotional strains between Emily and Charlotte. Charlotte's indiscretion in reading the Gondal poems when she found them lying open on a table is more damaging to the sisters' friendliness in Mrs. Gérin's account than in others. There is no doubt about Emily's reserve, her hesitation about publication. Still it seems worthwhile to remember that she did help with the preparation of the book of poems and its failure did not deter her from pressing on with her novel *Wuthering Heights* nor from sending that to a publisher and even writing him about her work on another novel, never finished and now lost.

Mrs. Gérin is very interesting in her presentation of Emily's feeling for Branwell—the most dramatic and deep emotion of her life if we have pieced that life together properly. Quite convincingly, she thinks that Emily's awkward, difficult nature, her own inability to find a life for herself outside her father's house, made her more sympathetic with the defenses and failures of her brother. Whether the sympathy, the tacit acceptance of responsibility for Branwell came from the absence of other claims in her life we cannot know. His sufferings over Mrs. Robinson were taken at face value by the family, anxious like himself to have some frame into which to put his appalling indulgences, his decline into delirium tremens and utter debilitation of body and spirit. They were willing to believe that his had been a fatal love, a curse.

Emily Brontë's life was as narrow as she could make it; her effort was to reduce her daily prospects and she had far fewer friends than Charlotte. She was away from home only four times: twice in boarding school, once as a teacher, and later in Brussels with Charlotte. All of these "experiences" were painful and abandoned with eagerness. Some of the trouble lay in her unbending nature. She was "stronger than a man, simpler than a child." There was no hope, in Emily Brontë, for conventional feminine behavior, plausible attitudes and manners. In certain ways she seems more damaged and suffering than her sisters, more doomed to solitude and to an inwardness somewhat frightening.

The blindness of the critics to *Wuthering Heights* is perhaps not an unexpected adversity for a work of such brilliant, troubling force. It was called "a disagreeable story," and pronounced "gloomy and dismal." Another reviewer wrote, "We know nothing in the whole range of our fictitious literature which represents such shocking pictures of the worst forms of humanity." When the strength and newness of the book were acknowledged, its power was called "a purposeless power." Charlotte Brontë was perplexed by it and in her introduction to a new edition printed after Emily's death said, "Whether it is right or advisable to create beings like Heathcliff, I do not know: I scarcely think it is." The unremitting tension of *Wuthering Heights* was at variance with Charlotte's mixture of romantic elements and didactic realism.

The last years of Emily Brontë's life are distressing to think about. Her writing stopped and nothing remains from the years 1846 to 1848, when she died at the age of thirty. It is not known whether she destroyed her papers or whether Charlotte, too much bound by her own clarity and reasonableness, judged the unprinted papers not worth preserving. Mrs. Gérin believes Emily's "voices" disappeared. Her work, leaning more upon inspiration than that of her sisters, less subservient to the dominion of the will, might well have slipped into a pause at the end.

There was also her draining dedication to Branwell. "Long after all the Brontë family were dead Emily's goodness to Branwell in his degradation was still village talk. Stories abounded of her waiting up at night to let him in and carry him upstairs when he was too drunk to walk." Branwell was like a pestilence. He slept all day and stayed up half the night raving. Once he set the bed on fire when he was deeply drugged. "Happening to pass his open door and see the flames, Emily shot down to the kitchen for a ewer of water, before anyone else had recovered from the shock or been able to rouse the supine Branwell." After this the father took Branwell to sleep in his room.

When Branwell died, there was immediately an inexplicable downward rush to death for Emily also. She had, according to all reports, been healthy, but she never went out again after Branwell's funeral and three months later she herself was dead. During the interval she spoke hardly at all, would not give consideration to her failing body. Charlotte was appalled by "the great emaciation, her breathlessness after any movement, her racing pulse . . . her exhausting cough." Emily refused medical care, yielding only to Charlotte's frenzy of fear on the last day. When the doctor finally arrived she was dead.

Charlotte's account of Emily's death is intensely moving:

Emily's cold and cough are very obstinate. . . . Her reserved nature occasions me great uneasiness of mind. It is useless to question her; you get no answers. It is still more useless to recommend remedies; they are never adopted. . . . Never in all her life had she lingered over any task that lay before her, and she did not linger now. She sank rapidly. She made haste to leave us. I have seen nothing like it; but indeed, I have never seen her parallel in anything.

There may have been a suicidal feeling in Emily's essential nature. In her poems and in her novel, death appears more perfect than life; it stands ahead as the ultimate liberty and freedom. "Thou would'st rejoice for those that live, because they live to die. . . ."

*   *   *

When Mrs. Gaskell was preparing her life of Charlotte Brontë she went to Brussels to call on the Heger family. Mme. Heger refused to see her but she spoke with M. Heger and, so it is thought, saw the love letters Charlotte had written him. She did not record either the feelings or the letters in her account of Charlotte, even though the falling in love, the extreme suffering endured because of this love were central experiences in Charlotte Brontë's life and in her work. Perhaps Mrs. Gaskell had given her word not to reveal the contents of the letters; more likely it was her own feeling of respect for Charlotte, solicitude for the "image" that made her wish to glide over the whole thing softly and swiftly. This left room for later diggers, and the love affair gets all the attention from them that it failed to receive from Mrs. Gaskell.

Winifred Gérin's biography gives the fullest account we have of the years at the school in Brussels. The suppressed and then recovered letters are interesting above all as a picture of the pitiable emotional strain endured by a young, inexperienced girl in her efforts to make a life for herself. For the rest, the story of Charlotte Brontë's letters is like some unfortunate, fantastical turn in one of her own plots. They are very earnest, agonizing documents, overheated, despairing, and intensely felt.

The existence of the letters is itself strange. We are told that M. Heger, supposedly entirely without fault or investment in Charlotte's passion, tore them up and threw them in the wastebasket. His wife, very brisk and firm in dispatching Charlotte when she sensed her infatuation, for some reason reclaimed the poor letters, thriftily pasted and gummed them together again. Mrs. Gérin has the odd notion that this was done for "evidence," but it is impossible to see the need for evidence in a case always presented as unilateral —that is, a deep, passionate crush on Charlotte's part for a man who had no interest whatsoever in her and gave her no reason to hope. In any case, in 1913 M. Heger's son presented the documents to the British Museum.

Charlotte and Emily Brontë went to Belgium to study French and other subjects in order to prepare themselves for their destiny as teachers. Emily stayed only one year, and when their aunt died, went home gladly in order to run the house for her father. Charlotte returned for a second year to the Pensionnat Heger, where they were studying—going this time as a teacher of English rather than as a pupil. In her decision to return, an anxious fascination with M. Heger certainly played a part, perhaps even the whole part. She wrote about it: "I returned to Brussels after Aunt's death, against my conscience, prompted by what then seemed an irresistible impulse. I was punished for my selfish folly by a total withdrawal for more than two years of happiness and peace of mind."

Falling in love with M. Heger laid the ground for the emotional intensity and recklessness in Charlotte Brontë's novels. She experienced to the fullest a deep, scalding frustration. The uselessness of her love, the dreadful inappropriateness and unavailability of its object, turned out to be one of those sources of pain that are also the springs of knowledge. Her misery caused her to examine her whole life, to face what lay ahead; and if she found little to be optimistic about, at least she knew how to think deeply, and in a new way, on the condition of loneliness and deprivation. This was important because the condition was then and is always shared by so many. Her familiarity with it was awful.

Reprieve came with the success of *Jane Eyre* and her other books. This novel and the later one, *Villette,* are powerful images of nineteenth-century female feeling. Lucy Snowe and Jane Eyre encourage at every point an identification with Charlotte Brontë herself. The two governesses are orphans, a prudent way of establishing the depth of their desolation. Anne Brontë's novel *Agnes Grey* is somewhat unusual among governess stories in that the girl has both her parents and sets out on her work to help deteriorating family finances. Most governesses in fiction are strangely alone, like sturdy little female figures in a fairy tale. They walk the roads alone, with hardly a coin in their pockets; they undergo severe trials in unfamiliar, menacing places and are rescued by kind strangers. Shadows, desperation, and fears are their reality, even if they go in for a litany of assurances of their own worth and sighs of hope that their virtues will somehow, in some manner, stand them in good stead.

At the Pensionnat Heger in Brussels, Charlotte Brontë— alone, proud, disturbed in mind—was thrown into the middle of an unbalancing family life. She could no more have resisted falling in love with the husband than Branwell could have denied the presence of Mrs. Robinson. At the Heger establishment life was heightened by the fullness and diversity of the responsibilities the couple had undertaken. There were children, domestic engagements, pupils, a school to be run; serious work for both husband and wife as teachers and managers; an important role in the life of the town; relatives, roots, bustle, worries, newness. Charlotte entered this life as if she had suddenly walked upon a stage and begun acting out a part whose limits and privileges had not been decided. One moment she was a family member; the next she was an excluded, ignored employee, a visitor from a foreign country.

In *Villette,* Lucy Snowe suffers a nervous breakdown when she is left alone in the large, empty school at vacation time —an insensitivity perhaps on the part of the family, but one not always easy to avoid. In real life, during the second year at the school, Charlotte Brontë seemed to have suffered the same lonely anguish and frustration as her heroine, the same sense of abandonment. In the book and in life, the undertow of hysteria and threat was very real.

When she returned to Brussels as a teacher in the school, Charlotte Brontë felt the improvement in her position as a pleasure. Her advancement was further enhanced by the beginning of English lessons in the evening for M. Heger and his brother-in-law. There is no question that the teacher greatly liked this new sense of power and accomplishment— and she cherished the pupil as much as the trust. The wife soon sensed, in the way of wives and headmistresses, the disturbances and storms of an infatuation. The lessons were stopped. This enraged Charlotte Brontë for every possible reason. First it underscored her powerlessness: *that* no amount of intelligence, skill, or hard work seemed to alter. The lessons represented self-esteem, competence, and a chance to be near M. Heger.

In the situation at the Pensionnat, Charlotte is very much like one of her heroines: a poor, clever teacher, rushing to fall in love with the master. The world the governesses inhabit, in the novels and in life, is a place of exclusion. These observant, high-minded, emotional women are desperate in the midst of a worldly social comedy that does not for a moment take them into account. Anne Brontë is thought to have fallen in love with a gay, flirtatious young curate, William Weightman, but this love was a secret suffering, a mute, hidden torment.

Poverty is the deforming condition in love, as the Brontës see it. Poverty makes you unable even to admit your love; in *Villette* poverty turns Lucy Snowe into Dr. John's confidante and pseudo-sister; it is unthinkable that he should have romantic interest in her even though he obviously values her highly, but merely in a restricted, excluding manner. During Mr. Rochester's flirtation with the shallow Miss Ingram, Jane Eyre assesses her own values and yet can only express them in a negative evaluation of her rival. About Miss Ingram she thinks:

She was showy; but she was not genuine; she had a fine person, many attainments, but her mind was poor. . . . She was not good; she was not original. She advocated a high tone of sentiment; but she did not know the sensations of sympathy and pity. . . .

Sympathy, pity, intelligence, goodness, genuineness—these are the charms Charlotte Brontë wishes to impose. There is something a little overblown in the heroine's hope to press virtues upon men who are conventional, and even somewhat corrupt, in their taste in women. The heroine's moral superiority is accompanied by a superiority of passion, a devotion that is highly sexual, more so we feel than that of the self-centered and worldly girls the men prefer. (This same sense of a passionate nature is found in George Eliot's writing.) Charlotte Brontë's heroines have the idea of loving and protecting the best sides of the men they are infatuated with: they feel a sort of demanding reverence for brains, honor, uniqueness. Mr. Rochester, M. Paul, and Dr. John in *Villette* are superior men and also intensely attractive and masculine. Girls with more fortunate prospects need not value these qualities but instead may look for others, money in particular. That is the way things are set up in the novels.

When she arrived in Brussels, Charlotte Brontë was twenty-six and M. Heger was thirty-three. His wife was a few years older. The school, from the evidence of *Villette,* was a battleground of sexual conflict, intellectual teasing, international and religious contraries, and feminine competition. It was a stimulating and unnerving scene. Unconscious wishes drifted through the halls.

Anything irregular in men fascinated Charlotte Brontë. Leslie Stephen may say that "Mr. Rochester has imposed himself on many," but the fact is that Rochester is a creation of great originality and considerable immoral charm. He is a frank and sensuous man for whom the author feels a helpless admiration. He has had a daughter by a mistress and many other affairs. He has an insane wife up in the attic and yet he proposes marriage, or rather marriages, once to a selfish and ridiculous creature and then to Jane Eyre. Of course the idea of a bigamous alliance must be forsworn and Jane flees; still the notion is a beguiling one and has pressed up through the dream life of the author. She had thought of every maneuver for circumventing those stony obstructions of wives who would not remove themselves.

At the Pensionnat Heger, the lessons stopped, trouble grew between Charlotte and Mme. Heger. Mrs. Gérin believes the wife, according to the convention of Europeans, cleverly, quietly worked to isolate Charlotte and to contain, without scandal or disruption, her overwrought emotions. If we can project the actual wife into the fictional creation of Mme. Beck, the headmistress in *Villette,* we can see that Charlotte had thrust herself against a powerful, interesting woman:

. . . looking up at Madame, I saw in her countenance a something that made me think twice ere I decided. At that instant she did not wear a woman's aspect, but rather a man's. Power of a particular kind strongly limned itself in all her traits, and that power was not *my* kind of power; neither sympathy, nor congeniality, nor submission, were the emotions it awakened. I stood—not soothed, nor won, nor overwhelmed. It seemed as if a challenge of strength between opposing gifts was given, and I suddenly felt all the dishonor of my diffidence, all the pusillanimity of my slackness to aspire.

The two women had some sort of quarrel. (Mrs. Gaskell offers religious difference; Mrs. Gérin insists that it was love for the schoolmaster.) Charlotte gave notice, which was, to her surprise, accepted even though M. Heger intervened and she finished out the term. Then she returned to Haworth and to a long frenzy of love and yearning. The suffering seemed to mount. She wrote letters and pitifully waited for answers. There were answers, supposedly merely advice on starting schools; when she later married, Charlotte destroyed the replies. The mood of the correspondence on her side is painful. "To forbid me to write to you, to refuse to answer me, would be to tear from me my only joy on earth."

The last appeal went out, delivered by the hand of a friend going to Brussels. Charlotte Brontë waited six months for a reply that never came. She had written:

. . . I tell you frankly that I have tried meanwhile to forget you, for the remembrance of a person whom one thinks never to see again and whom, nevertheless, one greatly esteems, frets too much the mind; and when one has suffered that kind of anxiety for a year or two, one is ready to do anything to find peace once more. I have done everything; I have sought occupations. . . . That, indeed, is humiliating—to be unable to control one's own thoughts, to be the slave of a regret, of a memory, the slave of a fixed and dominant idea, which lords it over the mind. Why cannot I have just as much friendship as you, as you for me—neither more nor less? Then should I be tranquil, so free—I could keep silence then for ten years without an effort.

Jane Eyre and Lucy Snowe are plain girls. They are touched by every disadvantage and must rely upon intelligence and a measure of ironical self-assertiveness to make an impression upon the world. They have dignity and make a trembling effort to hang on, even to win out. But how are they to do this? Both Charlotte Brontë and George Eliot are hard on the whims of beautiful women; it seems such a pity only pretty girls are able to win that fine, complicated hero the heroines and the authors would like for themselves. But women of intelligence learn resignation. Deprivation and renunciation are sisters. Susceptibility, emotionalism flare up, but duty and common sense and practicality finally keep disaster in check.

In Charlotte Brontë's novels a curious sophistication seems to be the property of the heroines without their even being entirely conscious of it. They understand certain worldly matters, especially those of a crypto-sexual nature. Lucy Snowe's thoughts on a painting in the Brussels museum shocked the novel's hero:

It represented a woman, considerably larger I thought, than the life. . . . She was, indeed, very well fed; very much butcher's meat —to say nothing of bread, vegetables and liquids. . . . She lay half-reclined on a couch—why it would be difficult to say; broad daylight blazed around her; she could not plead a weak spine; she ought to have been standing or at least sitting bolt upright. She had no business to lounge away the noon on a sofa. . . . Then for the wretched untidiness surrounding her, there could be no excuse. Pots and pans—perhaps I ought to say vases and goblets—were rolled here and there on the foreground; a perfect rubbish of flowers was mixed amongst them, and an absurd and disorderly mass of curtain upholstery smothered the couch and cumbered the floor. On referring to the catalogue I found that the reproduction bore the name, Cleopatra.

Humiliation is the companion of Lucy Snowe and Jane Eyre. The humiliation has to do with the insupportable greatness of their own responsiveness and the tendency of others simply to forget that these prying, analyzing recorders are just as alive and full of claims as they are themselves. For this reason there is a double-edged quality to the characters and this is part of the hold they have on our interest. Something about them is unexplained; they do not entirely understand themselves and they are, for all their brightness and energy, on the edge of nervous collapse.

Independence is an unwanted necessity, but a condition

much thought about. All of one's strength will be needed to maintain it; it is fate, a destiny to be confronted if not enjoyed. Charlotte Brontë's *Shirley* addresses itself to the regrets and consolations of lonely women, to the stoicism and patience they try to command. In her life and in her novels you are always dealing with a nettled complication of moods and traits, resolutions and lacks, ambitions and insecurities. The weight of family losses bore down upon her and there is actually something in her of an orphan, the condition she chose for her heroines.

Yet she was enormously energetic and her life was rich with friendships. *She* went back to Brussels and it was Emily who was pleased to stay at home. Charlotte's fictional characters are a defense of herself, of her qualities, and an embodiment of her fantasies. In life, at thirty-nine, she married her father's curate, a nice and devoted man for whom she felt little of the passion experienced long ago in the case of M. Heger. However, familiarity seemed to increase her husband's charms; she liked him better when she saw him in his youthful environment, with those he had grown up among and who cared about him. Then Charlotte Brontë came down with tuberculosis and the complications of pregnancy. She died, on the brink of domestic contentment if not romantic fulfillment.

The Brontë sisters have a renewed hold upon our imagination. They were gifted, well-educated, especially self-educated, and desperate. Their seriousness and poverty separated them forever from the interests and follies of respectable young girls. It was Charlotte's goal to represent the plight of plain, poor, high-minded young women. Sometimes she gave them more rectitude and right thinking than we can easily endure, but she knew their vulnerability, the neglect they expected and received, the spiritual and psychological scars inflicted upon them, the way their frantic efforts were scarcely noticed, much less admired or condoned.

How to live without love, without security? Hardly any other Victorian woman had thought as much about this as Charlotte Brontë. The large, gaping flaws in the construction of the stories—mad wives in the attic, strange apparitions in Belgium—are a representation of the life she could not face; these gothic subterfuges represent the mind at a breaking point, frantic to find any way out. If the flaws are only to be attributed to the practice of popular fiction of the time, we cannot then explain the large amount of genuine feeling that goes into them. They stand for the hidden wishes of an intolerable life.

Wuthering Heights is free of these failures because Emily Brontë did not think of the lovers in any usual domestic terms. Their feeling can never be consummated and brought down to routine and security. The novel is on a plane higher than those of the other sisters, since it is not bound by the daily, the ordinary—a thirst for the usual arrangements of life without the possibility of achieving them except as the result of outlandish interventions and accidents. Jane Eyre is always saving Mr. Rochester—when he falls from his horse, when there is a fire, when he is stricken with blindness. This is the circuitous path to dominance imagined by a luckless girl. *Wuthering Heights* is close to the regressive, to the anarchy of instinct; but Charlotte's books understand the need sometimes to fall back upon a dour superiority of mind and will.

All of the Brontë sisters carried about with them the despondency of their class and situation. We are astonished by what they would *not* endure. They rejected the servitude of fixed attitudes and careers, the slavery of poorly paid work; they resented the insufferable indifference of shallow people to the effort and exigency of those less fortunately placed. The sisters seized upon the development of their talents as an honorable way of life and in this they were heroic.

IBSEN'S WOMEN

A Doll's House

I BSEN COULD NEVER be agreeable for very long. He seemed to have the fat of choler in his bloodstream, all of it collecting there from a youth as bitter, homely, and humiliating as a man could endure. Fate kept this large mind and angry ambition working as a druggist from the age of sixteen to twenty-two in the freezing cold of the little town of Grimstad. Well-named. He was sore at his family because they were worse than poor; they had gone from being well enough off to a great diminishment—the kind of reversal that stood out like a birthmark in the nosy, petty provincial world of Ibsen's life, and of his plays.

The Ibsen family had to move from town to a miserable little farm on the outskirts. Father Ibsen had the inclination to bankruptcy and shadiness Ibsen used over and over in his work, and along with it the sardonic wit of a small-town failure who drank too much. Ibsen detested all of them, except perhaps his sister, and he himself suffered some of the hardness of heart of those who cannot come to terms with their families. Ibsen's mother, according to the biographer Halvdan Koht, started out as a sensitive woman who liked music and painting, but all her soul and energy soon sank into caring for her children and patiently enduring the bankrupt-prone father and his drunken-evening nonsense. It might be thought from Ibsen's interesting women characters that he felt some special love for his mother. It was not so simple as that. When his sister wrote that his mother had died, he didn't answer the letter for four months.

Still, he had learned everything and his ambition managed to feed on his own ill luck. In *Hedda Gabler,* Tesman says, "But, good heavens, we know nothing of the future!" and Lövborg answers, "No, but there is a thing or two to be said about it all the same." And so it is with Ibsen. He is guarded, protecting himself from too much feeling, and yet he had a thing or two to say about everything he had experienced. He seemed to have felt a troubled wonder about women that made his literary use of them peculiar, original, and tentative —like a riddle. His wife was devoted and constant and notably strong-minded. When her son was born she announced that was the end of it. No more! And so little Sigurd had no brothers or sisters. Ibsen pondered this without, so far as we know, strong emotion; he simply wondered what it might mean about his wife. His mother-in-law had been a novelist. There was a clear, Scandinavian, radical skepticism in the Thoresen family he had married into. For himself, Ibsen liked being away from the detested Norway, writing and writing, and getting a little drunk at night.

As he grew older and well known, fan mail came from the sort of young woman who yearned to attach herself to a famous man. Ibsen answered with more than the usual inanity; he met some of the girls. But again he was guarded; he didn't trust them too far and took a lot of it out in love notes. Emilie Bardach, the most important of these young girls, said her joy in life was taking men away from their wives. Ibsen was floored by this degree of ruthlessness. The "May sun in the September of his life" was a demon. Her demonism interested him, but in the end he could say, "She didn't get me, but I got her for my writing." Emilie was partly the model for the "inspiring" Hilda who attaches herself to the aging architect in *The Master Builder.* She sent Ibsen a photograph of herself signed, "The Princess of Orangia," a pet name used in the play. The great man was greatly annoyed. That was overstepping. The photograph was burned.

A Doll's House was naturally taken up by the women's rights movement. At first this was agreeable, but Ibsen couldn't in the end resist a put-down. He made an address before the Norwegian Society for Women's Rights and said he didn't know what those rights were. He cared only for freedom for all men.

The plays are about writing, disguised as architecture or sculpture (ambition for greatness), about provincial narrowness and hypocrisy, bourgeois marriage, money, hereditary taints of all kinds—from syphilis to the tendency to get into debt. He had obviously learned all he needed from Grimstad: bankruptcy, anger, the torments inside the little parlors of Christiania. And there was a large, steady poetic and dramatic energy that kept him going day after day, year after year.

Ibsen's realistic plays are somewhat different from those of his followers. His psychology is close to the kind we are used to in fiction; character develops in an interestingly uneven fashion, moving a little this way and then a bit in another direction. His people are not quite fixed. They are growing, moving, uncertain of their direction in life. With this sort of personality, dialogue and selected dramatic conflicts cannot tell us all we want to know. We would like to go back with Hedda Gabler and forward with Nora Helmer. We feel a need for some additions to the surrounding scenery. The characters take hold of our imagination and vanish just as we are beginning to know them. The curtain goes down.

It is not a defect in dramaturgy; no, all of that is mastered perfectly. The trouble has to do with the sort of character Ibsen wanted to write about, particularly the women characters. Their motivation is true, but incomplete. Perhaps the fluid, drifting, poetic tone of Chekhov would have suited these women better. We would not have expected quite the same sort of resolution Ibsen's playmaking techniques demand. You look deeper into the plays and there are hints, little fragments here and there, stray bits of biography, detached, fascinating, and mysterious suggestions. We feel Ibsen himself created certain characters out of a musing wonder and a deep, intriguing uncertainty.

Studying his plays is unsettling in the profitable manner of the very best literature. You are full of questioning. Where are the mothers of Hedda and Nora? Both of these women have been brought up by their fathers. What about the *ménage à trois* so frequent in the plays—one woman with her husband and the family friend, the doctor or judge who comes over *every* evening? Or the house with the wife and another woman, a predatory, idealistic woman, full of devastating plans? Even in his general attitudes Ibsen is immensely complicated. You never know. There are breaks in his liberalism and social concern; and yet he never wavers in his contempt for business, the clergy, and the social hypocrisy of the Norwegian towns. He also hated the destructiveness of clean abstractions ("the ideal") when it was imposed upon the streaked and stained effort to survive.

Is Ibsen "our contemporary"—to use Jan Kott's phrase? He shared most of his subject matter with the prose literature of his time. There has always been, in addition, the special tie between nineteenth-century Norway and nineteenth-century America: the same galling, busy puritanism, the town life moving on the wheels of disgrace and scandal, drunkenness and deceit. Think of the provincial character of the agonies: the neighbors, one's position in the town, the accountability for everything, the necessity for prudence and the temptation to excess. Some of this scenery has vanished and what is left may be broken and cracked, but neighbors and families and gossip, boredom, marriage, money, and work are still what the drama of life is about.

There has been recently an accretion of interest in the women characters in Ibsen: in the plight of Mrs. Alving, the chaos of Hedda Gabler, the ambition of Rebecca West. These are all dramatically interesting portraits, but world literature offers more complex and richly imagined women. What newly strikes us about Ibsen may be just what we had a decade or so ago thought was stodgy about him—he sees women not only as individual characters and destinies caught up in dramatic conflicts but also as a "problem." He seems alone, so far as I can remember, in suggesting that he has given thought to the bare fact of being born a woman. To be female: What does it mean?

He worried about the raw canvas upon which the details of character were painted. First you are a woman and then you are restless, destructive, self-sacrificing, whatever you happen to be. No doubt there is some Scandinavian texture in all this, some socialistic brooding, something to do with the masterful Thoresen women in his wife's family, with his wife herself. Women seemed very strong to him, unpredictable; they set his literary imagination on fire and so he needed them, but he didn't want to be engulfed, drowned by new passions. He was not domestic and liked living in hotels and hired places in Italy or Germany, summering in cottages by a lake, writing, not necessarily needing the whole sweep of the feminine plan of house, permanence for possessions, roots.

What can *A Doll's House* be for us? Nora's leaving her husband can scarcely rivet our attention. The only thing more common and unremarkable would be her husband's leaving her. The last line, the historic "speech," is in the famous stage direction that ends the play. "From below is heard the reverberations of a heavy door closing." The door is the door of self-determination. We have some idea why it is at last opened, but why had it, before, been closed?

A Doll's House is about money, about the way it turns locks. Here is the plot once more. Nora Helmer is the charming young mother of three children. She has been married for eight years. When we first meet her she is full of claims to happiness, but it is rather swiftly revealed that strenuous days and nights lie in the past. Still the marriage has life in it and Nora thinks she is happy. Indeed she is on the brink of being happier—things have taken a good turn. Nora's husband, Helmer, has been a struggling lawyer, but it is typical of his character that the courage and aggressiveness needed to survive as a solitary professional are not quite suitable to his temperament. He requires the corporate frame. Helmer has just been named manager of the Joint Stock Bank. It is a promotion in self-esteem, in social position, best of all in money.

It is Christmas Eve, the tree is brought in by a porter and almost the first line of the play is, "How much?" Nora gives the man a crown and in her first exclamation of liberation says, "Keep the change!" This gratuity, this enlargement of possibility and personal expansiveness are the very sweetness of life to Nora. Her money worries have been overwhelming; natural generosity, pleasant extravagance have had to be sacrificed. True, the new money is still maddeningly not quite there. Helmer's increased salary will not begin for three months. No matter, Nora has bought presents for the family instead of, as in previous years, sitting up all night making the trimmings and the gifts herself. In a mood of hope and indulgence she nibbles some sweets her husband, true to our own dental beliefs, has "forbidden" her in the interest of sound teeth.

In his first exchanges with Nora, Helmer calls her "his twittering lark," and his "squirrel," his little "spendthrift," his "featherbrain." These are not insults—far from it. The words represent the coins of affection they have been living on in the lean days. But still we see right off that Helmer is prudent and Nora is eager for room in life, for spontaneity. "No debts! No borrowing!" the husband announces. But he loosens up a bit with the prodigal demands of the holiday season and counts out some bills for Nora. "Money!" she says, sounding the thundering chord. When she is asked what she wants for Christmas, she declares that she would like cash. Helmer finds the occasion to frown over her likeness to her father when it comes to spending; the husband believes in the inheritance of acquired characteristics, and while he adores his little wife, he can see she is not entirely free of genetic imperfection.

At this point a visitor is announced. The social world of Ibsen's plays is greatly restricted, enclosed in a narrow frame, cut off by the very geography of Norway; the long, dark winters make for social repetition, and there is a kind of solitude at the center of everything. When the bell rings and the eyebrows lift at the unexpected caller, it is, unless it be that odd member of the triangular mystery, almost sure to be an old school friend of either the wife or the husband. Everyone else you know is right there, so to speak. This small-town life has moral consequences always; the players live with the threat of trouble over the most petty matters. When Rosmer changes some of his theological ideas it is a scandal. Error or past dissipation casts a long, long shadow. Small towns always remember you when you were young; they seldom believe all the good things they hear you have done later, since you went off someplace else.

The visitor in *A Doll's House* is Mrs. Linde. She has arrived on Christmas Eve. Those who call upon school friends they haven't seen for years are in a state of emergency.

Something awful has happened out there. But in Ibsen's plays they receive a rather guarded welcome. No one has much to give; money, love, friendship come at a high price. This is a bourgeois world just hanging on, even petty bourgeois in the amount of money on hand. Most of the characters can claim only education and profession, not riches. Nora's husband has been made manager of the bank in the nick of time; Hedda Gabler's husband, Tesman, is a professor with very little money; her father was a military man who left nothing; Eilert Lövborg is poor; his mistress, Thea, is poor; Rebecca West in *Rosmersholm* is poor. Mrs. Alving in *Ghosts* has enough money, but disasters such as she has known are worse than poverty.

Mrs. Linde is a confidante, a device, rather thinly sketched, but in her outlines of practicality and heavy duties she is an interesting contrast to Nora. Mrs. Linde has come to town to get a job. Money has had its way with her since birth. Her father died and she gradually had to look after her mother and her younger brothers. She married at last, seeking minimal security, forgoing love. But ill luck dogged her still. Her husband died but not before his business fell into trouble. He left her without money and even without "a sorrow or a longing to remember." It had been a complete blank—and no pension at the end of it. She survived. Mrs. Linde is steadfast if somewhat depressed. She has always worked.

At this point Nora starts to reveal the real plot of the play. Hearing of Mrs. Linde's troubles, of her lifelong sacrifices, Nora cannot resist admitting the troubles she, the happy, lucky young wife, has known. She has got herself into a mess on behalf of those she loves and she is proud of her steady, if unconventional, efforts to extricate herself. Nora too has made decisions, borne burdensome consequences. Yes, she has a husband and "three of the loveliest children," but she has had to find ways, she has had to work—"light fancy work . . . crochet and embroidery and things of that sort"— and copying late at night. Her secret is that she took on nothing less than the responsibility of saving her husband's life.

Helmer, when they were first married, had lost his health in the struggle to survive in the harsh commercial climate of Norway. We have no reason to doubt that he might have died without a trip south, to the sun. The bitter Norwegian winters, the coughs, the lung disease, the bronchial threats are perfectly convincing. "How lucky you had the money to spend," the penny-worn Mrs. Linde says about their year in Italy.

Of course they hadn't the money to spend. Nora, without telling her husband, who would have certainly refused or vetoed the idea, had borrowed the money from the disgraced moneylender, Krogstad. This man had been a schoolmate of Helmer's, an admirer of Mrs. Linde's, a small-town embarrassment to himself and his family because he had at some time been guilty of forgery, had not actually been sentenced, but had lived on—forced into usury—with a small post in Helmer's bank and no position in society. Nora turned to Krogstad for her secret negotiations on the money for the year in Italy; she also forged her dying father's name to the note because she didn't know what else to do. But they had their year in the sun, her husband is well, and she has been scrupulously paying back the loan with interest all these years, doing "fancy work," and saving pennies from her household money.

Lies had to be told, but Nora never doubted that she had done something both necessary and honorable. Also, the trip to Italy was one of those necessities that happily coincided with the heart's desire. When she gets out her pretty costume and dances the tarantella in a Mediterranean celebration of joy, we see that in saving her husband's life she has had the best year of her own. "I seem the fool I am not," said Cleopatra.

Mrs. Linde speaks of being alone and childless and Nora cries out, "So utterly alone. How dreadful that must be!" And yet when Mrs. Linde faces her present situation, her mother dead, the boys raised and on their own, Nora suddenly says, "How free you must feel!" Mrs. Linde finds only "an inexpressible emptiness." She has no one to live for and yet "you have to be always on the strain." This woman has had a hard life of lonely work. She is thoroughly capable, even shows a talent for business, and Helmer is easily able to offer her a job in his bank.

Still, Mrs. Linde is a paradox, the sort of puzzle at the very heart of this play. She is capable and hard-working, but *she is not independent.* Nora is impractical and inexperienced, loves "beautiful gloves," and wants the house to be nice—she is also *intrinsically independent* and free-spirited. In the end she leaves her husband and her children in order to find herself, but it is not the final gesture that makes her free. Anna Karenina left her husband and her son, but she was tragically dependent, driven finallly by the torments of love to a devastating jealousy and to suicide.

Mrs. Linde, with her business experience, is prudent and conventional like Helmer. She tells Nora, "A wife can't borrow without her husband's consent." Nora thinks that is nonsense, a technicality. (In this conclusion she shows herself prophetic of modern American practice.) She is not, like Krogstad, dishonest and self-pitying. Instead she seems to enjoy the triumph of the borrowing and the struggle to repay. She has nothing but the most honorable intentions toward the money and the interest. Krogstad is a true forger, always wanting to make a leap without taking the consequences. He whines about his reputation. "All paths barred." It is strongly suggested that he would have been more respected if he had gone to jail. Instead he has somehow edged out of that but has not been able to push away the cloud over his name.

No one understands vice better than Ibsen. He knows what a Krogstad is like. The outcast does not care about reality, but only about fancy. Krogstad holds Nora's fate in his hands; the fact that she has almost repaid the money does not impress him. He knows about the forging of her father's name. Well enough. She must make Helmer keep him on at the bank, give him that little bit of respectability. And then suddenly the minor post is not sufficient. Krogstad begins to dream, a true forger's dreaming. He will not be a mere clerk; no, he must be Helmer's right-hand man and soon become the manager himself! This flamboyant soaring, done in only a few lines, is masterly. (Old Father Ibsen dreaming over his schnapps, no doubt.) In the end, Mrs. Linde and Krogstad decide to share the future. It is a case of supply and demand.

Helmer finds out about the borrowing and the forgery. He flies into a rage and nowhere shows the "miracle" of understanding or of male chivalry Nora had pretended to expect. He thinks she's a treacherous little idiot who can tear down in a moment of folly all a man has built up by his most painful efforts. When he sees that it may not all be revealed, that they can get by with it, his fury abates. But Nora has suffered a moral disappointment. Helmer is not only a donkey, but a coward as well. She makes her decision to leave him and her children because she feels she has been deceiving herself about marriage and happiness and must now learn what life is really about.

The change from the girlish, charming wife to the radical, courageous heroine setting out alone has always been a perturbation. Part of the trouble is that we do not think, and actresses and directors do not think, the Nora of the first acts, the bright woman—with her children, her presents, her nicknames, her extravagance, her pleasure in the thought of "heaps of money"—can be a suitable candidate for liberation. No, that role should by rights belong to the depressed, childless, loveless Mrs. Linde and her lonely drudgery. The truth is that Nora has always been free; it is all there in her gaiety, her lack of self-pity, her impulsiveness, her expansive, generous nature. And Nora never for a moment trusted Helmer. If she had done so she would long ago have told him about her troubles.

Nora kept her secret because she took pride in having assumed responsibility for her husband's life. She also kept quiet out of a lack of faith in her husband's spirit, a thorough knowledge of his conventionality and fear. Even as he is opening the letter that tells of the borrowing and forgery, *before he knows,* she thinks, Goodbye, my little ones. Of course her worst fears are true. Helmer behaves very badly, saying I told you so, and babbling on about her being her father's daughter. Had Nora stayed with him, we can imagine a rather full store of grievance would be in the closet. At the least Helmer would be eternally joking about her foolishness and looking into his wallet at night.

It is difficult to play Nora on the stage. Not that the role is demanding in the usual ways, but rather because of the intellectual and emotional distance this spirited young wife must travel. It is common to link the early Nora and the late Nora by an undercurrent of hysteria in the beginning of the play—a preparation of the ground by a sprinkling of overly bright notes, a little breathlessness and hurry. Hysterical worry will not connect the two Noras. Her panic is a fleeting thing, based upon reality. It has to do with the pressing practical problem of the odious Krogstad's determination to use Nora for his own dishonest purposes.

The hysteria, the worry will not open the door. The only

way the two can be reconciled is for the players and the audience to give up their idea that an independent, courageous woman cannot be domestic, pleasure-loving, and charming. If the play were written today, Nora would have left Helmer long ago. They are ill-matched. She has a gift for life and a fundamental common sense made falsely to appear giddy and girlish by the empty, dead conventionality of Helmer.

An exchange about debt: Helmer says, Suppose a catastrophe happened to a man and his family was left with a coffin of unpaid bills; Nora answers, "If anything so dreadful happened, it would be all the same to me whether I was in debt or not." She shows this sort of undercutting intelligence and genuineness throughout the play. Her mind has always been free and original; she is liberated by her intelligence and high spirits.

Strange that Helmer should want a doll's house and yet be so hostile to details of domestic creation. Over and over he leaves the stage with an air of insufferable self-love when there is anything to do with sewing or household affairs. In one scene he mocks the arm movements of a woman knitting. He flees from the presence of the children when they come in from the cold outside, saying, "Only mothers can endure such a temperature."

Nora's children—this is a hedge of thorns. Abandon Helmer, all right, but bundle up the children and take them with you, arranging for his weekend and vacation visits. Even in Ibsen's day one actress refused the part saying, "I could never abandon my children." Nora's love for the children seems real. The nurse points out that they are used to being with their mother more than is usual. Helmer, again lecturing about heredity, says lying mothers produce criminal children. Nora shudders, remembering her interest payments. The nurse she will finally leave the children with is the one who has raised her, but still the step is a grave one. In one of the most striking bits of dialogue between husband and wife, Helmer says, ". . . no man sacrifices his honor, not even for one he loves." "Millions of women have done so," Nora replies.

When Helmer says that she cannot leave her children, she might have said, "Millions of men have done so," and in that been perfectly consistent with current behavior. Nora seems to be saying that she cannot raise her own children in the old way and that she needs time to discover a new one.

Nevertheless the severance is rather casual and it drops a stain on our admiration of Nora. Ibsen has put the leaving of her children on the same moral and emotional level as the leaving of her husband and we cannot, in our hearts, assent to that. It is not only the leaving but the way the play does not have time for suffering, changes of heart. Ibsen has been too much a man in the end. He has taken the man's practice, if not his stated belief, that where self-realization is concerned children shall not be an impediment.

In William Archer's Preface to *A Doll's House* he had the idea that the woman who served as the model for Nora had actually, in real life, borrowed the money to redecorate her house! There is something beguiling in this thought, something of Nora Helmer in it. The real case was a dismal and more complicated one. The borrowing woman was an intellectual, a sort of writer, who had some literary correspondence with Ibsen. A meeting was arranged and the biographer, Halvdan Koht, says that "she was hardly what he [Ibsen] expected, but young, pretty and vivacious." She was invited to Dresden, and Ibsen called her "the lark." Some years later the lark married and borrowed money secretly to take her husband south for his health. She had trouble paying he money back and the Ibsens urged her to confess to her husband. She confessed and he, in fury, demanded a divorce.

The poor wife suffered a nervous breakdown, was sent to an asylum. "In this catastrophe the marriage was dissolved."

The play and the true happening are a wonderfully rich psychological comment on each other. When we learn that the model for Nora was intelligent and ambitious everything falls into place. There is no need to wonder about motivation or changes of character, sudden revelations. Ibsen has not made Nora a writer, but he has, if we look carefully, made her extremely intelligent. She is the most sympathetic of all his heroines. There is nothing bitter, ruthless, or self-destructive in her. She has the amiability and endurance that are thetclues to moral courage. Nora is gracious and fair-minded. Even when she is leaving Helmer, she thanks him for being kind to her. With Dr. Rank, the family friend, who is in love with her, she is honest and her flirtation has none of the heavy cynicism of Hedda Gabler's relation with *her* family friend, Judge Brack, and none of the bitter ambitiousness of Rebecca's relationship with Rosmer. Nora is not after anything and we cannot imagine her in nihilistic pursuit of an architect *(The Master Builder)* or the sculptor *(When We Dead Awaken)*. Nora's freedom rests upon her affectionate nature.

The habit is to play Nora too lightly in the beginning and too heavily in the end. The person who has been charming in Acts 1 and 2 puts on a dowdy traveling suit in Act 3 and is suddenly standing before you as a spinster governess. If the play is to make sense, the woman who has decided to leave her husband must be the very same woman we have known before. We may well predict that she will soon be laughing and chattering again and eating her macaroons in peace, telling her friends—she is going back to her hometown—what a stick Helmer turned out to be. Otherwise her freedom is worth nothing. Nora's liberation is not a transformation, but an acknowledgment of error, of having married the wrong man. Her real problem is money—at the beginning and at the end. What will she live on? What kind of work will she do? Will she get her children back? Who will be her next husband? When the curtain goes down it is only the end of Volume One.

Because Nora is free and whole she does not present the puzzling tangle of deceit and subterfuge, suppressed rage and dishonesty, that are so peculiar a tendency in the women in Ibsen's other realistic plays. *A Doll's House* is a comedy, a happy ending—except for the matter of the children. The play was published more than ninety years ago and we have found out very little we could add. In the case of grating marriages the children are still there, a matter of improvisation, resistant to fixed principles. Fortunately some of Ibsen's more far-out heroines—Hedda Gabler, Rebecca West, and Irene—are childless and this makes their suicides and falling off a mountain easier on the moral sensibilities of the audience.

$\mathscr{H}edda\ \mathscr{G}abler$

HEDDA GABLER is one of the meanest romantics in literature. She is not offered as a grotesque or meant to serve as
a subsidiary who will force forward the plot and provide
comparison to those of a lighter, kinder spirit. She is, instead,
given the very center of the stage; she is given that by Ibsen,
and the ambivalent attractions of her nature draw our atten-
tions even closer, inside, toward those empty spaces neither
she, nor we, can fill with motive and purpose. Hedda is
mean-spirited and petty in both large and small matters.

The only other romantic figure of a corresponding hardness and cruelty is Heathcliff in *Wuthering Heights*. He does
not pretend to any courtesies or disguise. Still Heathcliff is
somewhat, if not entirely, redeemed by his annihilating attachment to Cathy, by his having been abandoned as a child
and cruelly tormented by the natural son of his adopted
father. Also, Heathcliff shows a sort of progress; he goes
away and makes a fortune, thereby indicating that for all his
sufferings there is a masculine force and control in him. He
gradually, by will and ruthlessness and again by control,
gains the Earnshaw property—but, of course, he loses in the
end all that could have made his life meaningful.

Creatures of the will move step by step toward victory and
loss almost at the same time. At least, this is true in literature

where design and completion play a part. Such persons will not allow for the contingencies of existence. The speeding will would destroy everything around it if it were not that the demands of aesthetic structure finally cut down the fascinating, offending, dominating hero. Like Heathcliff, Hedda Gabler attracts us and repels us at the same time. They are both, so to speak, stars, created figures, large but somehow without symmetry. We do not know where we are with them and often they are simply exaggerated, unimaginable creatures who fling themselves and their moods at us in a random fury. And yet their stories stir us; they are never boring. There is never a relaxation of tension. Something of universal psychic life and truth draws us to believe them as possibilities, even if we cannot connect them clearly and definitely to their actions under the terms of realistic causality. Restlessness, mood, obsession. Everything comes at us in fragments, disturbing bits and pieces. You feel life cannot sustain their degree of willfulness, and part of the suspense of their character is the anxious waiting to learn in just what way they will fall.

Hedda Gabler is unusual, I believe, in having no motivation whatsoever. In a sense, we do not want her defined. She is irksome, troubling, and yet a sort of heroine one is still investigating, pondering, at the end of the play as much as at the beginning. Her faults are profoundly deep and murky, stirring about in the darkest, coldest springs of destructiveness. She cannot like anyone, except perhaps her dead father, but she is a temptation, very special, like the Serpent, chosen by nature, by some casual stroke of fate, to represent threatening, willful, beguiling coldness.

Hedda has nothing in common with Medea, Phaedra, or Clytemnestra. They have been hurt, betrayed; they are jealous; they know love and therefore the need for revenge on its deceits. They have desires for the future, if only the desire to have destroyed certain conditions of the past. Their actions connect with their feelings. Hedda Gabler shares with Hamlet the quality of lending herself to a disconcerting number of possibilities for interpretation. But Hamlet's father has been murdered and his mother has married the guilty uncle.

With Hedda there is nothing to start with. She is not the Queen of Thebes, the Princess of Elsinore or even of Ibsen's Christiania; she is, instead, to be understood as a provincial, somehow (again not quite clearly)) a compromised woman of twenty-nine, newly married to the foolish and unimpressive scholar, George Tesman. She enters the play at an odd point in her life; she is on the decline, stuck. Being married to George Tesman is, for her, a bitter resolution; it is the negative side of overwhelming, relentless fate. There is nothing awful and grand about it; indeed it is embarrassing. Instead of the ancient betrayals, deaths, murders, and jealousies, Hedda's drama is to have started life with recklessness, flamboyance, and to have ended up with a dud; she has when we first meet her just endured a honeymoon with a dazed, educated simpleton. It is unbearable; the very atmosphere immediately announces not a tragic unhappiness but an empty, paralyzing, ridiculous marriage. The curious modernity of the plot is that the workings of destiny have shrunk to yawning boredom. We feel George Tesman is too good for Hedda, but no woman in the audience could possibly be in love with him herself. Difficult to place sympathy as the scene unfolds.

Hedda takes every chance to act badly and to hurt others. Sometimes she does so with a languid pettiness and sometimes with malignant determination. By nature all ice and indifference, she accomplishes her delinquencies without a rush of agitation or beating emotion; and that is why it is hard to remember that throughout Ibsen's four-act play Hedda does not show a single, decent, generous impulse. We consider her at her best when she shows nothing beyond her style. How is it possible that with all these distressing qualities, Hedda Gabler challenges and pleases and is the most fascinating, humanly interesting of Ibsen's women. Actresses long to play the role and she has had a steady public since 1890. The blurring, the murkiness of her bad nature are themselves dramatic discoveries. The audience, when it is a woman, knows her own George Tesman; and the male is ever willing to risk his peace with a Hedda.

Hedda Gabler is not operatic, except perhaps at the end. Before that, she is working out a small-town provincial destiny that takes place entirely in her own feelings and temperament. There is no political or philosophical content to her destructiveness; no angry raging against poverty, fate, injustice, ill luck. The obstructions again are negative: Who else? Where else? What else? she asks and there is no answer. Negative forces are more devastating to Hedda's integrity than positive wishes unfulfilled. This is the originality of Ibsen's extraordinary force in this work. The gods have not had their sport with Hedda. She has, if anything, had her sport with the gods. She has done as she pleased, without remorse, without thought for the suffering of the others. But even that is negative. Nothing whatsoever is advanced by her actions—for her. Others are woefully hurt, ruined, even killed, but she is not one bit richer or happier.

There are two corpses at the end of the play and, of course, that of Hedda Gabler herself is one of them. And yet the play is not in any true sense a grand tragedy. It remains a brilliant and brutal scene from provincial life, one that grips us with its dramatic fascination and yet does not leave us stunned by grief and pity. Some of the diminishment of emotion at the end of the play may be laid to Ibsen's decision to tidy up for us. Hedda has burned a precious manuscript and a promising young thinker has died of a gunshot in a brothel—these are

losses that might create waves of feeling in our minds. But
the loss is re-found. In the end Hedda's husband, Tesman,
and the young man's mistress, Thea, are sorting out the notes
from the dead Lövborg's great book, and sorting out themselves at the same time. A tragedy would not leave Thea and
Tesman with their life's work ahead of them up in the study.
After all, they have lost the persons they loved and their
consolation in a bit of editing and repasting for posterity is
more than a little dampening. And what about the effect of
the dramatic, offstage final gunshot, as Hedda shoots herself
cleanly in the temple? It is a memorable denouement about
which one feels not sadness so much as *Bravo!* Admiration
for skill and crazy daring and ultimate, complete indifference.

Hedda Gabler is a strange play, about a stranger. What is
wrong with her? Everything is wrong with her morally. She
has no particular virtue to recommend her, but she does have
an advantage, the advantage of style. This is what over-
whelms us, captures and holds our attention, makes us feel,
even unwillingly, a sort of complicity, admiration. Hedda is
cool—in the older sense of the word. She is not, by the
exercise of control, disguising turbulence and ambition, or
even need. Her indifference is real. She is not in love. No one
in the play has deeply stirred her feelings. The failure or
inability to care for anyone is the first condition of her nature. It is not, however, a cause of action; it is merely a
condition, the first circumstance of her character and her
situation. It takes its place along with other details, many
other details, such as being a liar. It is the basis of her style,
the very stuff out of which the image she casts has been put
together. It is intensely interesting.

Many terms have been used to describe Hedda, among
them "hyperesthesia"—a term suggesting some derange-
ment of sensibilility. And also a kind of anesthesia—frigid-

ity. There is something too hopeful in the use of any sort of medical or physiological determination of Hedda's character. It would seem to make us mourn that she had missed the felicities of "treatment" or simple sexual knowledge of the kind supposedly easy to come upon in our own day. We cannot know. We do know that she is a narcissist—a more ancient disposition, utterly tenacious and enduring. Yet the odd thing is that she is not particularly introverted or self-analytical. There is not much pleasure in her self-love. It is of an unproductive, even a useless, sort and so in the end she looks into the mirror endlessly and yet does not feel ardor for what she sees there. Again it is negative. She is merely more in love with herself than with anyone else, but not greatly in love.

Egoism erases Hedda's concern for others without giving her any transcendent joy in herself. She is wholly destructive, but not paranoid or schizophrenic. Indeed, she is something of a rationalist, a skeptic, and romantic posturings do not change her life. She doesn't expect things to turn out well, has little faith in finding a savior. How different she is from her old school friend, Thea, who has suffered every wound from life and yet is full of belief, belief in art and thought, in love, in the possibility of reclaiming a dangerously unsteady soul like Lövborg. Hedda, on the other hand, would seem to have been born knowing that Lövborg would not stay sober forever and would somehow put terrible obstacles in the way of writing his book, even of living out his life.

Another interesting thing about Hedda is that although "alienated" from purpose, she is mindful and perhaps even respectful of all those little conventions that decorate the surface and keep one safe. In the long run, again unlike the romantic Thea, Hedda knows that the conventions are simply too much trouble to break. And you would have to have a reason, a reason of passion, which she does not have.

She speaks of her own boredom, but what does that mean? Boredom does not designate a positive condition; again it is negative, merely a lack of whatever would not be boring. And again it is striking that Hedda's boredom does not improve her, does not make her long for something outside herself, something purer, deeper than the society of the scenery of "the west end of Christiania."

Hedda is not hysterical. It is natural that actresses would wish to find an objective expression for the mystery of Hedda's nature. They cannot merely *stand there,* delivering her brilliant lines. They wonder what she is like alone, in private. And there it is usual to imagine her being more frank with herself than with others. Alone, face to face with whatever she is face to face with, she is likely to moan and wring her hands, to *show* her inner distress, her desperation. This is wrong for Hedda just as it is meaningless for Nora. The hysterical gestures so often seen in the acting out of Ibsen's heroines are a way—secretive, on the sly, as it were—of trying for a clear and neat motivation the author does not wish to provide. Hysterical feeling and silent desperation create a sympathy, a surrounding of attractive feminine weaknesses, pitiable, searing, but not very serious. It would seem to be the only motivation we can imagine embodying. Alone, what would Hedda do? Nothing, perhaps. She is immensely idle and the idle do not wring their hands.

The play opens on a room in dark colors. Ibsen has specified that and it may represent something or merely be the fashion of the time in which he wrote. The drawing room is "spacious, handsome, and tastefully furnished" in dark colors. It leads to a garden with "autumn foliage." Hedda is not domestic. In Christiania, in the life of the Norwegian house, the family, this itself would perhaps be a striking circumstance. In this particular instance she is well contrasted to Nora, with her love of things, of dresses, ribbons, Christmas trees, special gifts for the children. They are both extravagant, but in a quite different way. Hedda's extravagance has no connection with herself. She does not know the bills, as Nora does, and so lets others borrow for her. She is, actually, the object of extravagance. Unknowable, mysterious, unrooted as she is, it is natural that simple, earnest people like her husband and his aunt would imagine that she could be identified, warmed, humanized by a proper setting. She has expressed a tepid desire to be, in the lack of any other occupation, a town hostess. But it is clear that Hedda could not accomplish this with her own social energy. It would require money and Tesman, her husband, does not have it, although he shows his suppressed knowledge of the foolishness and coldness of their marriage by stretching his finances to his own vague and humiliating idea of what would make Hedda love him. Things will not make Hedda love him, and in any case those Tesman can buy are never enough. The sacrifices made for her are painful in their inadequacy and in the awful cost to those who sacrifice. The dramatic point of the apartment so pitifully created for Hedda is the portrait of her father, General Gabler. He looks on from the adjoining room, more important than any other piece of furniture or expenditure could possibly be.

Hedda is returning from a wedding trip of nearly six months with her husband. Tesman is an unworldly man, very much the absent-minded professor. He is not a dark, voluminous Casaubon, as in *Middlemarch,* but a nice, middling Ph.D., rather dilatory about finishing his dissertation. Tesman is slightly ridiculous, and spectacularly without sex appeal. His is one of those disconcerting natures compounded of the blind innocence that protects him from knowing what he does not wish to know; if he is good it is not actively so, but is instead an expression of a soft and fuzzy self-protectiveness.

The man Hedda Gabler has married is much more of a girl that she is. She has been reared by a general on pistols and horses. He has been protected, brought up by women, two loving, self-sacrificing maiden aunts. His good old servant, another female parental figure for him, is now brought in to work for Hedda. All of these worn, old, thrifty, recessive ladies have loved their clean, innocent, A-student George. But in a way they are more worldly than he. They show a rational worry about his marriage to Hedda Gabler. It is as strange to them, as to us, that she would have chosen George Tesman.

The truth is that Hedda did not choose George. She says she "had danced herself out" and speaks without much conviction of Tesman's rather bare respectability and his lean future hopes. "And then, since he was bent, at all hazards, on being allowed to provide for me—I really don't know why I should not have accepted his offer?" Tesman's blind foolishness is not even redeemed by an overwhelming passion for Hedda. He seemed to have drifted into the marriage out of a sort of stumbling vanity that allowed him to believe that he, a dry scholar without even a professorship, was, in winning the reckless, restless daughter of General Gabler, simply doing something natural.

There is very little pathos in George Tesman's feeling for Hedda Gabler, and that is one of the most interesting things about Ibsen's vision in the play. This is one of those dim, loveless marriages on both sides. When Hedda kills herself, Tesman cries out, "Shot herself! Shot herself in the temple! Fancy that!" She is a stranger to him. The truth about her is that all of her suitors, including Judge Brack who is still on the scene, were attracted to her but aware that there was something deeply menacing to happiness in her nature. She is not marriageable. What, except personal charm, can she offer? There is vitality in her but it is all horses and shooting and emptiness. She does not move forward, go deeper, with anyone. Even with Lövborg, who in his own recklessness had tempted her to feeling, she will not admit that there was love at the bottom of their seductive friendship. "No, not quite," she says.

George Tesman is too inexperienced and too cut off from appropriate feelings to size up these things. He has been doing his dissertation on "Domestic Industries of Brabant during the Middle Ages," and that study did not teach him to back off from Hedda. Instead, he goes on trying to believe that disaster is good luck, that debts and indifference will vanish. The only hope he could reasonably have hidden in his mind is that the heartless Hedda would gradually show herself to be like the other women he had known—the devoted, sacrificing, adoring old aunts and nurses. There is something almost sordid in Tesman's willful inanity.

Hedda's first act of meanness is brilliantly conceived in its lack of necessity and in the depth of its pettiness. This skillful scene is the kind that gathers great rewards from the realistic rules of dramaturgy: the author places a cue, leaves it, and then suddenly pounces upon it again. We know that Miss Tesman, George's beloved aunt, has bought a new bonnet in honor of the returning bridal couple. The smallness, the pettiness of the insult Hedda hurls at the new bonnet are a measure of her meaningless cruelty. The old aunt can ill afford anything new, having signed away and mortgaged everything, including her annuity, for the furnishings of the villa. She puts her new hat on a chair as the play opens. Hedda spots it and turns upon it with indignation as an unsightly intrusion; she pretends that it must belong to the old servant. This is disgusting and we have not even the excuse that it might have been unintentional, since Hedda later admits it to be the kind of compulsion she is given to.

"Well, you see —these impulses come over me all of a sudden; and I cannot resist them."

Interesting characters enter Hedda's gloomy parlor. She is suddenly visited by Thea Elvsted, a school friend. Thea has had the narrow, bitter time of a nineteenth-century girl without means. She is attractive, fair, a little younger than Hedda —and desolate. Her first words are anxious ones, about despair, having no one to turn to. Her history is the miserable one of intelligent women, serious, penniless, thrown back upon the stingy, uncertain offerings of chance and the meager, degrading work of a governess. Thea had taken such a position as governess, deep in the country, hired to serve the children of Sheriff Elvsted. As it turned out, the wife was an invalid and Thea fell from the position of governess to that of housekeeper, all of it lonely and loveless, and without any kind of future. The wife died, and in hopelessness she married Sheriff Elvsted.

One of those opportunities for transcendence suddenly changed Thea's nothingness to the most joyful promise. She meets Eilert Lövborg, an old "friend" of Hedda's, school chum and gifted competitor of the pedestrian Tesman. Eilert is a thinker, an artist, a bohemian, a sort of Nietzschean figure whose career and accomplishment have been spoiled by drastic drinking. Thea falls in love with him. But it is more than romance; it is a mission, a sacred trust, one of those dedications that challenge the very essence of a superior woman. Lövborg is more than a romantic man; he is the instrument through which Thea can find some purpose for her own intellectual possibilities. She is a sort of graduate student; she believes in learning, in writing, in art, in culture. The flames of a passionate collaboration consume her. To live with Lövborg, keep him from drinking, help him to bring into actual being the books he has wanted to write: this mission absorbs her whole heart.

Lövborg, in the loneliness of isolation, seems to find himself. He quits drinking—that temptation so fiercely real to men of the northern countries and intensely so to Ibsen himself early in his career. Lövborg writes one book that is a success and has started upon the Real Book of his life, something much greater and more important to him. Of course, Lövborg's success with his first book has consequences. He has, artist that he is, come back into town to enjoy the fruits of it. He is not the same ruined man who lived and wrote in the sheriff's district. Work has reclaimed him. He can show his face once more and can even resume his right to challenge poor Tesman's hope of a professorship. Thea is terrified of the opportunities for delinquency provided by Lövborg's visit to Christiania. She knows her man. With daring and in desperation and knowledge, she simply flees from the home of her husband, to follow her mission, to save Lövborg once again. He needs saving.

The play develops with great skill. Lövborg had been infatuated with Hedda some years before. This we believe, as we cannot quite believe in the fate that made Hedda the wife of Tesman. Lövborg and Hedda have certain temperamental surges of impatience and restlessness in common. They are curious about life, attracted to danger, and Lövborg is quite frankly disgusted to find Tesman and Hedda as man and wife. He sees it as the farce it is. As for Hedda, the new fame, the "reclamation" by the less flamboyant, devoted Thea, the present book and the future book: all of this acts upon her like a poison. In the coffin of her life she wants amusement; she likes to brush against risk and danger; she feels a compulsion to overturn the reclamation, the accomplishment, the future.

Hedda taunts Lövborg into drinking, into taking the first sip that will lead to the second. In this scene Ibsen shows a true and piercing psychological realism. He understands Lövborg's powers of mind, the appeal of his nature, but he also knows the petty workings of self-justification, the ignoble turns of self-indulgence. Lövborg, like most alcoholics when they decide to start up again, looks for someone outside himself to blame for his sudden determination to enjoy himself once more. He finds an excuse of miraculous trueness.

Hedda tells him that Thea had rushed to town out of fear for the wavering of his resolution. She explains that Thea's anxiety for him rests upon the danger that he will take up his old habits and ruin his chance for fulfillment. The idea of being watched over, cared for, suddenly seems to him an imposition, a violation of his rights to ruin. He finds himself wounded, outraged by Thea's sensible lack of faith, by her constancy, her daring dedication to his sobriety. Lövborg lifts his glass and says, "To your health, Thea!" It is no wonder Shaw called him "a male coquet."

Lövborg gets drunk, loses his manuscript, ends the night in a brothel. The surest workings of conventional plotting take a miraculous turn at this point in the play. Instinct and device merge and a strange violence, a rush of anarchy, flows through the scenery. Tesman had found the manuscript and brought it home, but when a ravaged, desperate Lövborg turns up the next morning Hedda does not tell him that his book is safe. Instead, when he threatens to destroy himself out of disgust with his life, she hands him one of her pistols and makes the odd, unforgettable plea: "Eilert Lövborg—listen to me. Will you not try to—to do it beautifully?"

Hedda slowly puts the manuscript into the stove, saying that she is burning Thea's child. Among other brutal feelings that take over Hedda's mind, one of them seems to be a protest against romanticism, against the expansiveness of Lövborg's ravings about what the book had meant to him and to Thea, how precious it was, how it stood for life, for fidelity, and for love.

As a general's daughter, Hedda has aesthetic notions of

marksmanship; she believes that guns should be used with style. But Lövborg is a writer, an intellectual, driven by rages of remorse, despair, and uncontrollable feeling. He has all the awkwardness, the clumsy carelessness of his kind. Yet, even with that, his end is truly a mess, full of outrageous horror, and no elegance at all. At the brothel the pistol in his breast pocket discharged and the ball lodged in his bowels. "That too!" Hedda says, with an expression of "disgust." "Oh, what curse is it that makes everything I touch turn ludicrous and mean?" The absolute dreariness and ineptness of her existence seem to be illuminated by Lövborg's ludicrous death. We do not know what she wished of him, except that in some way she wished to be the agent, if only the agent of destruction, in someone's life, someone outlandish enough to be worthy of her own outrageousness. Hedda shoots herself in the temple—properly. She is at the end as at the beginning all style, but style without a proper setting. It is finally just a series of gestures, isolated, drifting. Thea and Tesman hope to piece the lost book together from notes. Even that destruction is conditional, imperfect.

George Brandes speaks most interestingly of the "coarseness" of the world in Hedda Gabler. He writes, "Even where the conversation is carried on in a kind of masonic slang that is not lacking in wit, it is devoid of all refinement." In the translations available one cannot get all the sound and rhythm, the social overtones, but there is no doubt about what Brandes means. This is one of the fascinations of the play—the undercurrent of vice and corruption. Judge Brack is an oily, sly sensualist, with the kind of knowledge of life offered by a clever cynicism. There is indeed something legalistic about his nature—he is mindful of details and in this capacity is a sort of blackmailer. He likes the quiet, sly drama of "situations." His stag parties end in drunkenness and verge on the sordid—even the timid Tesman does not come home until dawn. Nevertheless, we feel Judge Brack is always in control, watchful, a bourgeois—and that is part of the "coarseness."

Madame Diana's boudoir, where Lövborg is killed, appears to be a natural plank in the social structure. Most interesting of all is Hedda's floating curiosity about the underside of life. She and Lövborg have had long conversations, revelations. "There I would sit and tell you of my escapades —my days and nights of devilment." She confesses that she wanted "a peep, now and then, into a world which she is forbidden to know anything about." Actually, Hedda has a thirst for experience—combined with a self-protectiveness that keeps her in line. So in the end very little is open to her, neither the thrill of recklessness nor the comfort of respectability.

But it is not Madame Diana, stag parties, and loose recollections that make for the coarseness. It is the moral and intellectual shallowness of Hedda, her arrogant coldness, and ignorance. Her determination to destroy the worthy, loving, serious Thea, for no reason or gain to herself, comes from a nature not only damaged but fundamentally low. Her jealousy of Thea is not new, even though it has not in the past, nor in the present, been based upon a genuine competition. It is Iago's destructive compulsion, rooted at one moment in a triviality, and at another in something more threatening but never adequate to the destroying impulses. There is a waywardness in her never to be explained, and yet it does not seem unreal, incredible. Hedda is real enough, tangled, knotted rather than truly complex. We cannot find the force in her that might have prospered under a different sun because her force, her presence, are very much contained in all those defects and compulsions out of which Ibsen has created her. She is not the flower of environment, but rather of inner essence.

Ibsen's stage instructions describe Hedda as having hair of an agreeable "medium brown, but not particularly abundant." Thea's hair is "remarkably light, almost flaxen, and unusually abundant and wavy." This accounts for the remembered instance in their school life when Hedda tried to burn Thea's hair. Also it is curious that when she is burning the manuscript Thea has helped Lövborg to write, helped him so much they sentimentally call it their "child," Hedda speaks not of Lövborg but of Thea, and again of her envy of Thea's hair. "Now I am burning your child, Thea. Burning it, curly-locks!" This is the envy and emptiness of a narrow, vulgar world.

One of the main clues to Hedda's character is that she is a Philistine. For all the rage of her temperament and the glow of her recklessness, she is the general's daughter, a child of the military life. Philistinism in her has a certain aristocratic coloring of defiance and arrogance, and she would not fit Arnold's use of the term for that reason. But she is not an aristocrat; she has neither practical means nor the assurance that certain openings into pleasure and comfort can always be found. Her daring is that of specialists—in this case the military—and it does not suffice in the absence of duties. She is truly rootless without her father, classless, without definition, adrift. To set oneself up against the claims of culture and creation without having worldly privileges to take their place causes great turmoil in the unconscious. Envies, angers, and aggressions churn and fuss and yet it is hard to feel superior to culture and learning without having extraordinary natural assets of another order. Defenses are devious and distaste for real worth is justified as proportion, judgment. A cold and controlled Philistine like Hedda will always see in sentiment about art and creative effort a general sentimentality and exaggeration. Poor Thea, in telling of leaving her husband to follow Lövborg, of going to his rooms to look for him—actions a respectable woman of that time could not easily take on—keeps saying, "What else could I do?" This sort of *activity* on behalf of another—even on behalf of love—this intense engagement, the social risk, the bother are incomprehensible to Hedda. Selfishness and Philistinism combine powerfully in Hedda's nature. She despises those acts of dedication that fill the void.

First, she is contemptuous of Tesman's running about in the libraries of Europe on their honeymoon. True, his projects are not exalted and he is a nervous pedant. But would it not have been the same to her if he had been studying Baroque churches or the French Revolution, if he had been writing poetry like Wordsworth? To Hedda, unworldly concentration is absurd. She would rather buy a favorite horse than have Tesman buy books on his special subject. "Your special subject?" she says, as if she did not even remember what it was.

Hedda is as much interested in Lövborg as it is possible for her to be interested in anyone. Yet, when her husband brings in Lövborg's new book and asks if she wants to look at it, she says, "No, thanks." When she burns the manuscript she is showing her contempt for the intellectual effort that went into it. In confessing the destruction to Tesman, she speaks of it as "only a book." And if Lövborg is foolish enough to kill himself over the loss, well, "Do it beautifully."

At one point Hedda has the idea that her bumbling, shy, bookish husband should go in for politics. The cynical, worldly Judge Brack is astonished that such an unlikely thing should occur to her. Of course, she hardly thinks of Tesman as likely to succeed as a minister. What she reveals in the suggestion is the idle working of a mind that can think of any outlandish matter, since she has a fundamental contempt for what Tesman is doing, what he can do, what he has always done—his earnest, uninspired scholarship.

The emotions Hedda arouses in us are tentative, ambivalent. She is the center of our fixed attention and yet we do not know how to feel toward her. Her style and the fascinations of her futile indifference are strong enough to suggest that longings for her nature if not her fate are in all of us. We cannot pity her because of her lack of any instinct for goodness, her disregard for the claims of other people's lives; and yet her carelessness with her own life is a perverse form of honor. She is coarse and, worse, soulless, but the cool, cynical wit of many of her best scenes tells us that she is not stupid.

Is she more a man than a woman? Perhaps so. Her only joys have been horses and guns. She treats her husband as if he were a bad colt picked up at an auction. Her coquetry is guarded, not very different from the masquerades of the bachelor Judge Brack. Neither is overcome by romantic impulse; they will not go under for love. The idea of becoming a mother is unbearable to Hedda. But her peculiar Philistinism—the destructive form it takes—has something to do with the fact that the only life she has is a woman's life of the most reduced sort. True, the reduction is due in part to the perversity of her character, to her refusals, omissions, deviations. She has no projects that engage her, she has never been asked to cultivate an understanding of intellectual and creative concentration, to experience the pleasure and labor of it.

Hedda Gabler is a bourgeois woman of the nineteenth century. What is odd about her is that in sloth and disaffection she has turned away from the props and crutches by which other women desperately tried to give life hope and warmth. She has no respect for what is called "a woman's world" and even less for a life of work and ideas. The cave of nothingness which she has gradually entered seems to leave only a dull resentment alive. She can at least partici- pate, slyly, in the civil war of one woman against another. She is a foot soldier in this battle. Hedda is always contemp- tuous of women and cruel to them when the occasion arises. She is mean to the servant, indifferent to the death of the old aunt, wicked to allow Miss Tesman to pauperize herself to furnish the unloved villa, and, most of all, sadistic toward Thea. If Hedda may be said to have loved only her father, her only other surviving emotion is hatred of Thea. But why should she hate her, what is to be gained by it, what can it really mean to her?

Thea, the eternal student and nursemaid to talent, the depressed wife of Sheriff Elvsted, had little for Hedda to envy in the past except for her fund of patient survival energy. But this energy has become something glowing and useful when it attaches itself to the damaged artist, Lövborg. It is genuine and it is radical. The energy and feeling are insistent enough to give Thea the courage to leave her husband and to set out, in the classical, illuminated, isolated way of a hero, to pursue her fate. She sees in the backsliding, special Lövborg, a cause, a belief, a love that could truly identify her as a person, a life. Thea is not dominating in the play, not deeply interesting or ever able to invade the center of our feelings. She is an idea, historically another Nora, without Nora's charms. Her gove- rnessy, high-minded qualities stir up a heated hatred in the feckless life of Hedda; it is the hatred of the arrogant, not of the driven. That is why it is dry and futile.

Hedda's recollection of her jealousy of Thea's abundant, curly hair is a symbol of a trivial, enduring envy, one of Ibsen's marvelous, throw-away insights. We pity Hedda that with her the winds of experience and purpose, or simply the activities of life, have not been able to sweep away this rem- nant, this discreditable scrap of youthful greed. Her destructive courage and style have not, after all, left her free of the slaveries of girlhood.

When it first appeared, *Hedda Gabler* received the worst press of all Ibsen's important plays. The objectivity, the distance, the refusal of doctrine, the mysterious, menacing *scare* of it, the lack of "womanly" qualities in a character so riveting sexually and dramatically—hardly anyone was immediately able to see the desolate grandeur and foretelling of the creation. Hedda, rather than Nora, was the real prophecy. Hardly a woman in, for instance, the films of Ingmar Bergman is imaginable without her.

The Rosmersholm Triangle

Thus on the fateful banks of the Nile,
Weeps the deceitful crocodile!

Rosmersholm is one of Ibsen's most interesting plays. The surface is clear enough and yet the darkness is very thick and troubling. Like so many of Ibsen's plays, there is no one in it to like without ambivalence. This lack of a positive is seldom troubling; here it is the murky negative that disturbs us most sharply. Which of the three can one trust? How is life to be served here—and whose life? It is a play about death perhaps, the death of the hunter, in this case a woman, who returns from her trip into the forest of sexual competition with two bleeding carcasses and a feeling of futility.

The heroine, Rebecca West, is a fiercely engaging woman. She is recognizable, especially in her acquaintance with dilemma, the dilemma of survival. She is torn apart by the kind of high motive she wishes to offer life and the decision and the low passion and cunning by which these high dreams are to be accomplished. The ugliest necessities and the most splendid hopes toss her about in a manner of the greatest dramatic and psychological interest. Early deprivation has sharpened her intelligence, hardened her will, without in any way making her freely accept the immorality of private selfishness or social inhumanity. She must entrap, and then must step on the sharp blades herself.

The play has Ibsen's usual atmosphere of petty social construction, the sort of suffocating, entangling environment that unites the despair of place with the despair of feeling. Coldness and the bitterest heats of survival fight miserably with each other. In the background there are dirty politics and cowardly conventionality, but the essential action, the backward and forward movement of the plot, lies in the characters and the competive struggle between the two women.

When the play opens, the wife, Beata Rosmer, is dead by suicide, and Rosmer is left with the agent of the suicide, Rebecca West. The lovers are now free to take up life in the same spot, Rosmersholm, where all is the same, except that the wife has been removed like a touching but obsolescent piece of furniture. The wife's memory hovers about them, but her lingering is not of the sentimental kind, although the rather cozily set-up mourners at first try to pretend that such is the case. In truth, the dead wife had been the peculiar center of a harsh and demeaning power struggle. "It was like a fight to the death between Beata and me," Rebecca finally confesses. The play, beginning on the suicide of the wife, proceeds by way of revelations, compromises, and threats to the gradual circumstantial, psychological strangulation of the survivors. Rebecca and Rosmer are free, but they are led by the turns of their escape to seek death, to clasp hands and go the way of the wife, into the rushing waters of the mill-stream.

The resolution is not quite satisfactory on the plane of probability. The circle is closed too neatly. The lovers' suicide, "imitative," as it were, is an extreme and unnecessarily corporeal finishing of a drama that is moral and psychological. Also, gross experience tells us that Rosmer and Rebecca will find a way to do as they please. The dead are gone. Whatever advantages the empty space may provide are likely to be swiftly occupied by the living. And yet the triangular struggle between the two women has been so fierce and primitive, the rewards of it finally so futile and empty, that we follow Ibsen right up to the mill bridge, even if we cannot easily concede the plunge into the waters.

Perhaps Parson Rosmer, the object of the two women's struggle, could wish the symbolic cleansing and expiation. He is one of those finicky, unsteady Ibsen men who need, above all, to like themselves. Rebecca West, the complicated heroine, is a different matter. She has been formed by the forces of necessity and will, traits that do not psychologically lend themselves to the suicidal resolution. Still, Rebecca has unusual self-understanding and it is this that ruins her victory over the dead woman. When she, too, goes the way of suicide, the housekeeper speaks the last line: "The dead wife has taken them."

Yes, the dead wife has taken the living, but only in an oblique sense. Disgust, futility, the final inadequacy of Rosmer are the devastating powers. The psychology of the play is at every point original and disturbing. The relationships are so complicated by guilt and evasiveness, by idealism in the service of personal, hidden gratifications of the ego that the play puzzles. Smoothness and violence mingle strangely. The turns and shifts of consequence are black, unexpected, but true to feeling.

It is Ibsen's genius to place the ruthlessness of women beside the vanity and self-love of men. In a love triangle, brutality on one side and vanity on the other must be present; both are necessary as the conditions, the grounds upon which the battle will be fought. Without the heightened sense of importance a man naturally acquires when he is the object of the possessive determinations of two women, nothing interesting could happen. If he were quickly, carefully to choose one over the other, the dramatic reverberations would be slight, even rather indolent. The triangle demands the cooperation of two in the humiliation of one, along with some period of pretense, suffering, insincerity, or self-delusion. In *Rosmersholm* the husband is unusually dense and mild. He courteously refuses to understand the drama that has exploded around him, to take in the violent sweeps of feeling in himself and in the two women. Rosmer leans as long as he can on the stick of "friendship" and "innocence" to protect himself from his love for Rebecca and his complicity in his wife's suicide.

The triangle in *The Master Builder* is more straightforward than the hesitations and longing of *Rosmersholm*. The aging builder finds himself surrounded by the willful, destructive young Hilda. The girl has attached herself to the distinguished man for a bit of sadistic teasing. Solness, the architect, is tormented, failing, and yet too vain to suspect the dangers of the young girl. He has, up to her entrance, been busy trying to emasculate his younger competitors, and this in itself is always a large, emotional drama for an artist. Solness is, as Shaw says, "a very fascinating man whom nobody, himself least of all, could suspect of having shot his bolt and being already dead." The architect's wife, Mrs. Solness, is dejection and depression itself, immobilized gloom, supposedly somehow sacrificed to the Moloch ambition. This we are not quite obliged to agree to because Ibsen has not made her appealing enough, not been able to imagine just what an artist's wife, or the wife of a man of great ambition, can do except be jealous, suspicious, and ill.

The victim grows, as a plant grows leaves, the foliage of dejection. Depression is boring, suspicion is deforming, ill health is repetitive. Our sympathies fall away and we can scarcely blame the husband who will naturally, in the gloom,

want light. It is interesting that in Ibsen's plays the wives are
as likely as the husbands to want the diversion of the young
woman who comes into the house. Two is not a perfect
number, and the childless, miserable wife fascinated Ibsen.
Hilda, in *The Master Builder*, actually occupies the empty
nursery on her visit of darkness. It is her role to inspire the
declining builder. "Higher and higher!" calls the awful
young girl. She waves her white shawl at the giddy architect
who has scaled the rafters and he falls to his death.

In *Rosmersholm*, Rebecca has come down from the
North. This freezing land of harshness and deprivation
leaves its mark on the spirit. There one learns the lessons of
life, the fears of poverty and isolation. (In *An Enemy of the
People*, Dr. Stockman remembers his span of service in the
North with a sense of the oppressiveness of life under the
conditions there. It is only the strength of moral conviction
that allows him to put his present, more hopeful circumstances in jeopardy and perhaps face a return to the cold,
soul-shrinking region.) Rebecca is thirty. She is intelligent,
emancipated, idealistic. Her youth has both tarnished and
hardened her. She is probably the illegitimate daughter of the
Dr. West who adopted her but did not offer her any special
kindness.

(Freud, in an anaylsis of *Rosmersholm*, believes that
Rebecca West had been the mistress of Dr. West, whom she
discovers during the play was her actual father, not merely
her adopted one. Therefore she has committed incest with
her own father, and her renunciation and suicide are an
expiation of this guilt as well as the guilt of her complicity
in driving Beata to suicide. Michael Meyer's imposing,
thoroughly achieved biography of Ibsen quotes the Freud
essay with appreciation. Still, I cannot find critics other than

Freud who thought Rebecca West had been the mistress of Dr. West. If this astonishing breach is indeed present in one's mind it will tend to overwhelm all other problems of the play.)

When Rebecca comes to Rosmersholm she is in a dangerous state. She is free—or, rather, adrift. She is immensely needy, looking desperately for some place to land, to live. And what can it mean for her, with her high-mindedness and her threatening need? It means she must have a husband, and soon. What else can she hope for? Again the narrow possibilities for poor, intelligent women in the nineteenth century define most of their choices, stage their drama. They are always looking for a way out, but something worthy, with content either social or artistic, is their hope.

Heaven is not likely to send a desperate, strong-willed woman of thirty an interesting, unmarried man. No, it will send her someone's husband and tell her to dispose of the wife as best she can. Wives accommodate because they invariably have their faults and their glaring lacks. These are transformed into moral issues and the defeat of deficiency becomes something of a crusade. Thus in righteousness is the hurdle vaulted.

The Rosmer family is a solid one, and somehow Rebecca attaches herself to it. Mrs. Rosmer, Beata, becomes fond of her and invites her to settle on the estate. Mrs. Solness, in *The Master Builder*, does not quite rise from gloom to joy at the sight of Hilda with her knapsack and alpenstock, but even she agrees to find a place for her. The torpid life at Rosmersholm and at the villa of the Solness family is such that these additions, naturally electrifying to the husband, are eventful puzzles and renewals to the wives as well. For change, vitality, everyone is willing to take the risk. This, once more, is a measure of the closeness of life in Ibsen's plays, the repetitive frustration of it, the oppressiveness of provincial attitude and society.

At Rosmersholm there is stagnation, but Rebecca soon sees little corners and cracks where inspiration might creep in. She sets about overthrowing what she decides to be, in Shaw's words, "the extinguishing effect" of Mrs. Rosmer. During her residence she calmly works at altering and liberalizing the views of Rosmer, who had previously been a parson and is now struggling with unorthodoxy. Rebecca does not try to brighten the conventional attitudes of Mrs. Rosmer, although there seems every possibility that, with a certain amount of effort, the sun of idealism might have been welcomed there also. The intellectual excitement—a genuine part of Rebecca's nature—has the most stimulating and happy effect on Parson Rosmer. But he is still prudish and needs the blanket of high intentions to cover their growing love, to make it appear to himself "good" rather than "bad."

Beata Rosmer is sensitive and high-strung. She is well aware of the way things are going, and where they will inevitably end. When the play opens Beata has already committed suicide. She has jumped into the churning waters under the mill bridge. Rosmer and Rebecca have had a year of quiet mourning, and if Rosmer still can't bring himself to walk over the bridge, there is no doubt that he is quite well, very much alive, and not inclined to vex himself with blame for his wife's suicide.

We learn about Beata's life and death gradually, as the play unfolds. In a tangled, small-town tussle over ideas, religion, and politics, the state of mind that led to Beata's self-destruction is gradually revealed. Her suffering had been immensely complicated, made up of jealousy, genuine love for her husband, and an early, numbing sense of defeat and helplessness in the contest with Rebecca. Beata had become so nervous and distraught that the lovers decided her mind had failed and this had been the more or less accepted view of her suicide, although there were those in town who had what everywhere are known as "their own ideas."

A year has passed since the death and things might have gone along well, except that in a political and theological dispute in the town points are scored against Rosmer by the revealing of a secret suicide letter in which Beata had absolved Rosmer and Rebecca of all blame for her self-destruction. Naturally, you cannot be absolved of something you are not accused or suspected of. Rosmer is forced by the absolution to connect Beata's sufferings with actions of his own. It is at this point that the psychological depth of the play is most moving. In brilliant shifts of feeling, the sadness and waste of the triangle begin to rot the relationship between Rosmer and Rebecca. Rebecca makes an astonishing confession. She acknowledges her ruthless humiliation of the wife. "I wanted to get rid of Beata, one way or another. But I never really imagined it would happen. Every little step I risked, every faltering advance, I seemed to hear something call out within me: 'No further. Not a step further!' . . . And yet I could not stop!"

This is the dead center of the play. Rebecca's self-knowledge lifts her far above the selfish teasing of Hilda, but it is worse also because she is older, better, more valuable in every way. She has committed one of Strindberg's "psychic murders," a horrible one with a real body washed up on the shore. What else could she do? She did it to live. Rebecca's will and necessity crushed Beata. Rosmer, and the possession of him, had become the possession of an important, life-enhancing commodity. The ethic of the struggle had been the business ethic—no ethic at all, except the advantage of profit. The parson is willed to change hands like a corporation, with the old, outmoded group being cast aside and the new liberal management quietly installed. At the opening of the play, we see Rebecca placing flowers about the drawing room, a nicety Beata never cared much for. Rosmer is shifting from the conservative to the liberal side of local issues. Those newly in charge are making changes.

When Beata was still alive she had ceased to be a person for the lovers and had become a mere negative. Things couldn't go forward when she was about, and what a wonderful force the parson might be if it were not for the drag of the past . . . But this is not at all true. It is self-interest that drives Rebecca and darting, smug self-satisfaction that allows Rosmer to pretend nothing is happening.

As the facts unfold, the rightness and sureness of Ibsen's sense of the contest never falter. First, the lovers deny Beata any participation in their interests and ideas. She is excluded on the grounds of her past dampening effect upon the advance of skeptical thinking within the household. We can imagine they would change the subject when Beata joined them and begin to talk of trivial, tiresome things or fall into bored silence. We are not sure that Beata was unworthy to help along the new day. She was fearful, but then she had sized up the importance of fresh ideas to Rebecca. Rosmer's sexual timidity, his need for innocence did not leave any other path open. Secondly, Rosmer took as proof of his wife's insanity the fact that she had hysterical fits of passion for him, threw herself at him.

What can you do with a man like that? Of course, Beata was on the right track. Fear and rejection had told her all she needed to know. She saw that Rebecca meant to "have" him; they had closed their feelings to any claims of her own and it was all confused in her poor husband's mind with radicalism, atheism, and a delightful new friendship. Beata's character and her predicament, as it comes to us from the description of others, make her a plausible possibility for suicide. Rebecca's ruthlessness and Rosmer's dimness are an overwhelming force.

But in Ibsen things are never simple. When Rosmer at last faces his wife's jealousy, her anguish over his love for Rebecca, these new conditions, this new understanding of his own past, have the most peculiar effect upon him. He is immediately caught up in a fascination, even a sort of triumphant admiration of his wife's suffering. With a sudden flood of imaginative comprehension he puts himself in her place, goes through every step of her agony. "Oh, what a battle she must have fought! And alone too, Rebecca; desperate and quite alone!—and then, at last, this heartbreaking, accusing victory in the mill race!" He is deeply impressed by the ultimate quality of his wife's love, by the grandeur of her sacrifice of her own life. What can compare with this? he asks himself.

Rebecca urges him to forget the dead, to live, to move away from the past. But it is no use. Rosmer now announces himself fascinated by destruction, not by life. He and Rebecca have moved into darkness. They have begun to distrust and to dislike each other. Ashes are in their throats. Rosmer is frightened of Rebecca and in a Norwegian madness of his own asks her to match Beata's love. Together they throw themselves in the millstream. Even if the suicide is not entirely convincing, there is no life left in their love. But they do not die from guilt, but from the uselessness of it all, from the emptiness, from self-hatred.

What had Rosmer meant to Rebecca? She had the notion that she could, through him, accomplish a self-definition impossible by her own efforts. One would have to agree that in her situation and time this bright, penniless orphan could scarcely hope to enter history unattended. Her plans for an enlargement of views, for free-thinking joyousness and life-giving openness are merely longings of her personal temperament that have been ground into dust by poverty, lack of connections, the absence of any security or hope. What good does it do her to be "a new woman" until she has properly settled herself somewhere? And where is that to be if not at Rosmersholm?

Rebecca must, it seems, manipulate someone or fall by the

wayside. Her flirtation, even her exploitation of Rosmer would not trouble us—if only there weren't the wife. Beata is something like Nora's children. Sacrifices on certain terms disturb us. Rebecca's motives are, by force of circumstance, always paradoxical; fineness of spirit is mixed with the coarse determination to appropriate Rosmer, to sweep away his past obligations, to win out over someone else. It is a futility and harshness upon which nothing grand can be built.

What does Rosmer offer? He offers, most of all, comfort —and that is the bare truth of him. He is well-to-do, respected, has a margin of possibility because of his "ancient stock," and his pliable nature—a general eligibility. There, alone at Rosmersholm, with Beata out of the way, he and Rebecca would side with the liberals, slough off clerical repressions, bring in flowers and light, gracefully question the traditions: this would be the good life as Rebecca imagines it. If she doesn't "get" Rosmer, what will she do? She knows what lies ahead. She has not been asleep all these thirty years, and instead has a "past"—a miserable, dead love affair that gave her nothing. She *must* seize Rosmer and his acres. The element of absolute necessity gives her situation a strongly vital and insistent aspect.

Still, the lack of scruple is large and the consequences are ugly. Rebecca fights to the very end. When Rosmer begins to sink into his peculiar remorse she faces him with a direct question: Would you bring Beata back? Rosmer demurs, not able to accept the clarity and honesty of the challenge.

There is always something vulgar about a triangle. Even in the most elevated circumstances, the struggle is one of consumption, of "having" or "getting" something that is not, so to speak, on the free market. The victors are degraded by slyness, corruption, and greediness; the loser by weakness and humiliation. Heartlessness, ignobility, and ambition are the essence. It is a struggle for the experienced, not for the very young. Only those who have lived and endured have the understanding of the narrowness of opportunity within one lifetime. This experience provides the energy and the brutal decisiveness necessary to persist.

The critic A. C. Bradley, who has the most radiant appreciation of the love of Shakespeare's Antony and Cleopatra, nevertheless notes that Octavia, whom Antony married for reasons of political advantage, is wisely left in the shadows. "We resent his [Antony's] treatment of Octavia, whom Shakespeare was obliged to leave a mere sketch, lest our feeling for the hero and heroine should be too much chilled." Indeed every triangle is lowly and has, in the end, a diminishing effect upon the dignity of the man, just as it diminishes the moral life of the women.

Isn't Rosmer just a bit comic? He has been turned into an object by Beata and Rebecca. Observers on the sideline see everything about him that is hidden to himself, especially his fertile justifications. Vanity, boastfulness, emotional pomposity infect his thoughts and actions. He cannot in the end be taken seriously and this above all makes the bitter battle for possession stupid and ugly. After it is over, Rosmer will inevitably be overcome by a suspicion that something has happened to him he had not expected. Is he loved for himself? the object will finally wonder, just as the heiress is aware of the commercial value of her decisions. Am I worth dying for? the conscience luxuriously asks. The answer is No. Soon, all the joy—they have called it here the "innocence"—has gone out of the future. Rosmer is sensibly filled with fear of the conquering woman. Where did her ruthlessness come from? Has it died away forever, or is it only lying hidden for the moment?

Now he remembers that there was something large, exceptional, splendid about Beata's love. Why should he forget Beata's devotion to him and live completely in the new present? A love like that is an example, if nothing else, to the next one, a judgment, a comparison. It can be used.

We cannot help sympathizing with Rebecca because of her intelligence, her gift for life, and the unjust cramp of her circumstances. We are sad that she requires an object and a victim. Rebecca is not vicious like Hedda Gabler, but she is not devoted like Thea, either. Why shouldn't she have attached her idealism to the wavering conscience of Mortengaard, a newspaperman trying to pull up from unfortunate mistakes? After all, it has been said of Rosmer that "he never laughs." No, in Finmark she has known the hazards of disgrace and dependency too closely to have energy left for such extensive reclamations. Also, there is everything attractive, graceful, and promising about her. She wants the stage setting of her life to correspond to these possibilities. The question of her own birth likewise inclines her toward the power of the long accumulations of the Rosmer family. Rebecca is too exposed to be a bohemian and a crusader, she wants to be a patrician liberal.

The terms of a triangle are always exaggerated and distorted and its excitement is temporary. We know it will one day be settled; someone will give way, give up, step aside, die. When it does, letdown and questioning poison the victory. A struggle between two men for a single woman is a somewhat different construction. The man would rather not have a predecessor; the necessity of winning and displacing is irksome and degrading. How much better were she fresh, free, the fields unplowed. It is only the strength of desire that enables him to endure the embarrassment. There is even the sense that some natural bond with other men, a bond of fellowship or domination, has been broken. A woman, however, is not always sorry that there should be an open battle; if she wins it is a mark of her own powers, an achievement, a triumph. She expects to fight her way, for how could it be otherwise? Through him she is to live and no price is too high.

One feels that Vronsky, for all his love of Anna, would soon have backed away if she had not made their affair possible. But she is determined and so he tries to believe, with Antony, that "The nobleness of life is to do thus." Vronsky tells himself that only the old-fashioned disapprove of his conduct. He even gets his ideas into line, and because of the irregularity of his situation with Anna, "he has become a partisan of every sort of progress." Earlier, Vronsky allowed himself to think that Karenin was "a superfluous and tiresome person. No doubt he was in a pitiable position, but how could that be helped?" Inside Vronsky knows tht he too is in a pitiable position and he does not care for it. But he is trapped by love and Anna's obsession, as Rosmer will finally see that Rebecca's need for him was a trap.

The conflict in *Rosmersholm* is an *active* one. The three people are discovering each other, creating and destroying. This is, many feel, its own justification and morality. The characters are helpless in the face of a spontaneous happening that only slowly turns into a matter of possession and dispossession, ownership and loss. This is different from the deceit in *The Wings of the Dove*. Kate Croy and Densher are pure commercial principle without innocence or illusion, and so are Osmond and Mme. Merle in *The Portrait of a Lady*. These are sad, capitalist lyrics, ending on the dying note of all triangles: "We shall never be again as we were."

Ibsen withholds full approval and sympathy for Rebecca, just as Tolstoy withholds it from Anna. They do not believe women should live by the will, accountable only to desire. The heroines become distorted, destructive; a strange hysterical emptiness begins to cut them off from natural feelings. When Anna has a child by Vronsky she finds that "however hard she tried, she could not love this little child, and to feign love was beyond her powers." The kind of love she has for Vronsky is outside the scope of family life—for that even Karenin is better.

When Rebecca agrees to kill herself in the millstream it is not expiation but a furious disappointment in Rosmer and disgust with herself. Rosmer is perhaps ready for death, since he has fallen back in love with Beata, or with her love for him. Ibsen once said in explanation of *Rosmersholm:* "Conscience is very conservative." The trembling, uncertain fascination Ibsen felt in the struggle between the two women is the power of the play. He did not quite trust Rebecca and had himself experienced women of her sort. True, he was, as Archer describes him, short-sighted, of low stature, peering, thin-lipped, with a mouth "depressed at the corners into a curve indicative of an iron will."

No matter—he was also one of the most famous men in Europe and a particular excitement to girls and women in Germany, Vienna, and Scandinavia. "Miss B. is totally mad for Mr. I.," and "Miss B. is grief-stricken." Miss B. (Emilie Bardach) was eighteen and Mr. I. was sixty-one. He knew how determined poor thirty-year-old, brilliant Rebecca could be, and how inanely tempting the Nordic siren Hilda. But his plays are written out of suspicion, not infatuation. And perhaps that is why he understood so brutally the pathetic false hopes of the heroines that by possession and appropriation they would possess themselves. In that way there is a radical undercurrent to the realistic plays. If they have any moral it is that, in the end, nothing will turn out to have been worth the destruction of others and of oneself.

VICTIMS
AND VICTORS

Zelda

ZELDA FITZGERALD'S sad, wasted life seemed to have been buried beneath the ground, covered over by the desperate violets of Scott Fitzgerald's memories. It had gone by, we thought, interred in the mournful, expensive defeat of Fitzgerald's last years. "I left my capacity for hoping on the little roads that led to Zelda's sanitariums," he wrote. And why dig it up again? For it is a more than twice-told tale, capped by Ernest Hemingway's contemptuous epitaph in *A Moveable Feast*. There had always been about Zelda's collapse, even her death at last in a fire at a nursing home in North Carolina—"her body was identified by a charred slipper lying beneath it"—something of a reckoning, the price to be paid for recklessness beyond endurance, for drink and arrogance and carelessness with one's own life and that of those nearest. Or, perhaps, the reckoning, which was breakdown, insanity, was merely mysteriously there, compelling the earlier transgressions and excesses.

As persons, the Fitzgeralds were not, in my view, especially appealing. Their story has a sort of corruption clinging to it, the quality of a decadent fairy tale, some overgrown lushness and deformation. They seem, most of all, like incestuous brother and sister—brilliant, perverse, selfish—their handsome, self-loving faces melting into a mask. Sometimes they make one feel it is almost a deprivation to live without the correcting education of those common marital oppositions of temperament and taste.

In this couple defects were multiplied, as if by a dangerous doubling; weakness fed upon itself without a counterstrength and they were trapped; defaults, mutually committed, left holes everywhere in their lives. When you read their letters to each other it is often necessary to consult the signature in order to be sure which one has done the writing. Their tone about themselves, their mood, is the fatal one of nostalgia— a passive, consuming, repetitive poetry. Sometimes one feels even its most felicitous and melodious moments are fixed, rigid in expression, and that their feelings have gradually merged with their manner, fallen under the domination of style. Even in their suffering, so deep and beyond relief, their tonal memory controls the words, shaping them into the Fitzgerald tune, always so regretful, regressive, and touched with a careful felicity.

In nostalgia there is the pressure of ennui, and even the Fitzgerald youth, extraordinary, successful, special, so often seemed threatened by this backward-looking boredom and emptiness. This, along with evil circumstances and crippling vices, made the very existence of Fitzgerald's brilliant novels and stories a miracle. It was only at the end of his life, when he was composing the fascinating novel, *The Last Tycoon,* when he was tired and despondent but somehow, if only by time and fatigue and distance, free from the self-pity of his unproductive years, that he could subdue the half of himself that was Zelda. The mood of this last novel, not necessarily more interesting than the others by any means, was at least new and one felt a severing had been accomplished, an amputation, feared and longed for . . . But, as in a fairy tale, it was too late.

*   *   *

What then is the purpose of a biography of Zelda Fitzgerald (*Zelda,* by Nancy Milford) and a return to this thoroughly scrutinized marriage? Mrs. Milford is not very resolute as an analyst, nor is she a particularly interesting writer on her own. Still, setting out for the wife—the appendage, so to speak, the other side of the question—gives a peculiar vision, a different lighting to the stage. We cannot say that Zelda had ever been in the wings, in the dimness in any of the many Fitzgerald studies—this was scarcely possible for one so brightly noticeable. But Mrs. Milford has done something new. By concentration upon her subject, and even perhaps by inadvertence, she has brought troubling thoughts to our minds, shifted the balance of things, and made it possible for the reader to see in this unhappy woman—a fleeting paragon of the 1920s—an instance of unexpected moral complexity, an example of peculiar failure and the object of a kind of unnamable injustice—domestic, social, cultural?—and the victim of many miseries that were not always unavoidable. Of course, with Zelda it is well-known that many faults lay in herself and in her stars, but new to discover a frantic will to overcome them, a strong talent and intelligence struggling to live—and most surprising of all, incredible energy and longing for discipline. She appeared to experience the desperate creative urge that some have without even having an art. None of it was fully understood or valued by those around her, those in charge of her fate.

First, the vicious portrait of Zelda in Ernest Hemingway's *A Moveable Feast.* In these interesting chapters both of the Fitzgeralds are hit, like baby seals, by the hunter's club. Hemingway is smug and patronizing to Fitzgerald and urges upon us forgiveness by laying Fitzgerald's weaknesses and pains at the feet of his wife. Hemingway sees Zelda as a "hawk." She found him "bogus." In a memoir one would seem to be obliged to believe, to accept in the larger outlines, anecdotes recorded about distinguished contemporaries. Yet sometimes we cannot summon belief, since only the story-teller seems to be in his own skin. This is the case, in my view, with the demeaning anecdote in which Hemingway claims that Fitzgerald, humiliated, longing for reassurance, asked him to consider whether his "measurements"—Hemingway's title for this little memory is "A Matter of Measurements"—were adequate, since, he said, with great embarrassment and uncertainty, Zelda had told him he was not properly constructed to satisfy a woman. Hemingway took the poor questioner into the toilet, had an assessing look, gave a lordly verdict that all was as it should be, if looked at in profile as one gazes at statues in the Louvre, and that what was wrong was that Zelda, trying to put him "out of business."

It is very difficult for the mind to transport poor Fitzgerald, unzipped, to the WC—"*le water,*" Hemingway calls it—but not at all hard to imagine Hemingway falling into his role of sexual surveyor, measuring and judging. Another reason for some skepticism about the details of the memoir is the fascinating passage about Zelda at the end.

Zelda was very beautiful and was tanned. . . . Her hawk's eyes were clear and calm . . . she leaned forward and said to me, telling me her great secret, "Ernest, don't you think Al Jolson is greater than Jesus?"

In Mrs. Milford's book this memorable high-camp remark is spoken to Gerald Murphy: "Gerald, don't you think Al Jolson is just like Christ?"

Before her first breakdown, Zelda provoked extreme distaste and disdain among her friends and in the mind of her husband by taking up, after casual lessons in her youth, the determination to become a ballet dancer. This is a matter of great interest, because as it emerges in Mrs. Milford's ordering of Zelda's letters and statements and hopes, this new activity becomes more or less a model of the way in which her ambitions were forever to be viewed. Her desire in ballet study was profoundly intense and strained; it meant, as her letters show, many different things to her—release ("sudden fame," it was ungraciously called) and escape from alcohol, idleness, emptiness, and dependency. She wanted to have something of her own, as she said over and over again. The enormous discipline required to study the ballet was not a deterrent, but rather something that appealed to her. The story has been told many times, as an example of insanity, of Zelda jumping out of a taxi in the middle of the street in Paris, for fear of being late for her lessons.

The ballet obsession came after a particularly bad time of quarreling and drinking. Fitzgerald's attraction to the young actress, Lois Moran, and his taunt that "at least the girl did something with herself" are thought to have played a part. Zelda began lessons with Catherine Littlefield in 1927 in Philadelphia, but the work became much more important to her a year or so later in Paris when she was studying with Madame Egorova. She went about her ferocious study with "grotesque intensity" and a driven, outrageous energy. Her husband was not relieved and freed for his work, as one might have imagined, but vexed and angered by her concentration and likely to see it as a vengeance against himself.

What Zelda admired, loved even, in Madame Egorova was "her poverty and dedication." The intensity, the practice, the determination, became so extreme Zelda was put in a hospital in Paris, where her great thoughts were grief for the loss of "her work," for the example of Madame Egorova who had, she said, "given her the greatest possible joy." Later on, her psychiatrists at the hospital were enlisted in the battle to destroy Zelda's concentration and passion. The reasons were always curious ones, no matter what she tried. It was felt that since she couldn't be "great" as a dancer, a painter, a writer, it was damaging to try; it was necessary to control her pleasure in these activities. About the dancing and the doctors' opposition to it she said, "The light in which the thing presented itself to me was: I had got to the end of my physical resources. . . . If I couldn't be great, it wasn't worth going on with, though I loved my work to the point of obsession. . . . It was all I had in the world at the time."

With a deep feeling of having been wronged, Fitzgerald wrote, "After having worked all day at home, I would want to go out at night . . . my wife, on the contrary, having been gone all day, wanted only to stay home and go to bed." One of the natural results of the long hours of ballet practice was the near ending of Zelda's need for alcohol. This gratuity was not greatly considered by anyone, apparently, nor was the sheer advantage of the discipline itself, the joy she took in it, the glaring clarity of the good it might do in providing her not fame as a great dancer, but a milieu in which to live and to find work and satisfactions of some related kind. Instead,

Dr. Florel was absolutely certain that the way to Zelda's recovery did not lie in further dancing, and he too thought Scott should write to Egorova. But he suggested that Fitzgerald make clear to her their preference that in her answer she discourage Zelda, even if it was a gross deception.

(This was merely the first solicitation by husband and friends of a professional discouragement, sought for the victim's own good.)

They got their answer from Madame Egorova. It was far more positive than either of the men had wanted, but certainly less than Zelda would naturally have hoped for. It said what any observant, interested person could have seen for himself: she had started too late to become a first-class performer, but she had become by the sheer magnitude of perseverance and effort a good dancer and might have found professional work.

Zelda was diagnosed abroad by the distinguished Dr. Bleuler as a schizophrenic. She herself thought Dr. Bleuler "a great imbecile," but we have little reason to imagine other physicians would have been more moderate or hopeful in their predictions. Her mental confusion was sometimes alarming; she suffered, on occasion, disorientation, hallucinations, great fears and depressions, even to the point of a number of suicide attempts. But these low periods could not have been other than transitory because her letters throughout her illness are much too lucid, controlled, alive with feeling and painful awareness. She showed eccentricities, shifts of mood, odd smiles, nightmares, withdrawals, obsessive behavior—*at times*. At the same time, and much more to the point, is the lucidity, the almost unbearable suffering over her condition and her full recognition of it—and the most important and moving thing, an extraordinary zeal and strenuous effort to get well, be real, to function—above all *to work* at something. The latter desperate need is an astonishing desire and hope for one who had been a great beauty, who was the wife of a famous man, and who had lived a life of spectacular indulgence, along with *feminine* expectations of protection and love.

At her most ill an insight that was almost tragic persisted. She understood that something was wrong and that somehow she must pull out from under, by some strenuous effort of her own spirit. "I seem awfully queer to myself, but I know I used to have integrity even if it's gone now. . . . You've *got* to come and tell me how I was. Now I see odd things, people's arms too long or their faces as if they were stuffed and they look tiny and far away, or suddenly out of proportion." Almost worse than the mental suffering was a raging eczema that spread over her whole body, making it impossible to sleep. At times she was swathed in bandages from head to toe. These eruptions often followed a visit from her husband, and even periods of general improvement in her condition seemed, from the record, to coincide with his absence from her.

When they were still in France, Zelda was released from the hospital after a year and three months of treatment. Her case was summarized as "reaction to her feelings of inferiority (primarily toward her husband) . . ." She was stated to have had ambitions which were "self-deceptions" and which "caused difficulties between the couple." Fitzgerald, weary of his own guilt, was relieved to learn of a history of mental troubles on both sides of Zelda's family. When her brother committed suicide he said, "You see—it's not my fault—it's inherited."

His own drinking made him uncertain of his moral rightness. Zelda begged him to stop, but he resisted suggestions about this from such men as Dr. Adolph Meyer in Baltimore. He would fall back upon the complaint that Zelda was living on him, in every spiritual and material way. She was

. . . under a greenhouse which is my money and my name and my love. . . . She is willing to use the greenhouse to protect her in every way, to nourish every sprout of talent and to exhibit it—and at the same time she feels no responsibility about the greenhouse and feels she can reach up and knock a piece of glass out of the roof any moment, yet she is shrewd enough to cringe when I open the door of the greenhouse and tell her to behave or go.

In Zelda's fight against insanity and dependency she turned, as many disturbed people turn—the educated ones at least—to the hope of release through the practice of art. This hope rests upon the canny observation, clear even to the deranged and sequestered, that artists do not require the confidence of society to the same degree as other workers. And Zelda had lived since her teens with self-indulgent, damaged, and successful artists. There was a strangeness, not altogether promising for her, in the number of things she could do well. After her interrupted work in the ballet she turned often to painting, even though her eyes were not very good. In 1934 thirteen paintings and fifteen drawings were exhibited in Cary Ross's studio and there had been an earlier showing in the lobby of the Algonquin Hotel. Perhaps this exhibition was a curiosity more than anything else. An article about it in *The New York Times* shows again her enduring, passionate wish for self-reliance and personal freedom from dependency on others.

From the sanatorium last week which she temporarily left against doctors' orders to see a show of Georgia O'Keefe's art, Zelda Fitzgerald was hoping her pictures would gratify her great ambition—to earn her own living.

The very center of this study of Zelda Fitzgerald has to do, in a peripheral but interesting way, with literature, with her relation to her husband's work and to her own writings. Unfortunately for her, the most pronounced of her gifts was indeed for writing. And here again she has the precious gift of fantastic energy—not energy of a frantic, chaotic, sick sort, but that of steady application, formed and sustained by a belief in the worth of work and the value of each solitary self. She does not seem to have received any special dividends from motherhood, and domestic life scarcely engaged her interest for a moment. Early in her marriage, a friend, Alec McKaig, wrote in his diary:

Went to Fitzgeralds. Usual problem there. What shall Zelda do?
I think she might do a little more housework—apartment looks
like a pig sty.

Andrew Turnbull reports: "Once Fitzgerald told my mother
that there was nothing to eat in the house except five hams."

Zelda's greatest gift to Fitzgerald as a writer was her own
startling and reckless personality and his almost paralyzing
love of it. From McKaig's diary: "Fitz made another true
remark about himself . . . cannot depict how anyone thinks
except himself and Zelda," and "Fitz confessed this evening
at dinner that Zelda's ideas entirely responsible for 'Jelly
Bean' & 'Ice Palace.' Her ideas largely in this new novel [*The
Beautiful and Damned*] . . . ." Portions of her diary and her
letters had been used in *This Side of Paradise.*

When Edmund Wilson was listing the influences on Fitzgerald's work (Midwest, Irishness, and liquor), the author
said:

. . . your catalogue is not complete . . . the most enormous influence
on me in the four and a half years since I met her has been the
complete, fine and full-hearted selfishness and chill-mindedness of
Zelda.

John Peale Bishop's review of *The Beautiful and Damned*
felt that the fictional heroine did not come up to Zelda as she
was in life. Fitzgerald had not, he said, been able to get "the
hard intelligence, that intricate emotional equipment of her
prototype."

Articles and stories written by Zelda alone or by both of
them were sometimes signed by Fitzgerald for commercial
reasons. In 1924 Zelda had written pieces for *McCall's* and
"during the remainder of 1927 she worked energetically on
four articles, three of which were published the following

year. The first, 'The Changing Beauty of Park Avenue,' was signed by both of them, even though in his Ledger Fitzgerald gave Zelda credit for the article. . . ." In 1928 she began writing short stories. "Each story was written in an astonishing but hazardous burst of energy. . . . Five of these stories were to be published by *College Humor*. . . . Nevertheless, without exception the stories were published under both Fitzgeralds' names." At this time began Fitzgerald's preoccupation with "material," his odd conception that there was such a thing for fiction, independent of its embodiment in style, character, and plot. He thought these stories of Zelda's had "been pretty strong draughts on Zelda's and my common store of material." He worried about certain characters in the stories, "both of whom I had in my notebook to use."

They had created themselves together, and they always saw themselves, their youth, their love, their lost youth and lost love, their failures and memories, as a sort of living fiction. It does not seem of much importance that the dairies and letters were appropriated, the stories wrongly attributed for an extra $500. Zelda herself did not seem greatly concerned about any of this. She wrote a mock review of *The Beautiful and Damned* in the New York *Tribune* and said, "I recognized a portion of an old diary of mine . . . and also scraps of letters. . . . Mr. Fitzgerald . . . seems to believe plagiarism begins at home."

The real reason for Fitzgerald's worry about "material" perhaps had to do with the narrow nature of their lives and interests. They had beauty and celebrity and they went everywhere, and yet they were outside history for the most part, seldom making any mention of anything beyond their own feelings. Life, then, even at its best was an airless cell, and personal existence, the knots and tangles, the store of anecdote really counted in the long run. If there is any culpability on Fitzgerald's part it may lie in his use of Zelda's torment to create the destructive, mad heiress, Nicole, in *Tender Is the Night.*

Then, in the midst of insanity and incarceration, an astonishing thing happened. Zelda quite suddenly produced a finished novel, *Save Me the Waltz.* The drama around this achievement is disheartening and discreditable to everyone except Zelda. She did not consult her husband, but sent it off to Max Perkins at Scribner's—and the horror of the ballet lessons began all over again. "On March 14th Scott wrote Dr. Squires in a fury. He had just received Zelda's manuscript. . . ." For four years, he went on in self-pity, he had been forced to work only intermittently on his own novel, "unable to proceed *because* of the necessity of keeping Zelda in sanitariums. . . ."

There was an outcry about "my material," and Zelda revised or deleted the offending passages. Again, one of those heartless letters went out, asking that Zelda be discouraged from hope. "Then he asked Perkins to keep whatever praise he wished to give Zelda *'on the staid side'*" and went on to say—not quite truthfully so far as the record shows—that the doctors at Phipps did not want Zelda to be made to feel too jubilant about "fame and money." It was decided that she was too unstable for superlatives.

Save Me the Waltz is a novel of usual length, quite well written, drawing on Zelda's own life, and is thus a mixture of sharply observed Southern scenes and a contrasting worldliness. It is an entirely creditable effort, one that any new writer might be proud of and that any publisher would be sensible to offer, even though it was not a success when it did appear. That it was composed, hurriedly, by a "hopeless schizophrenic" is scarcely to be believed if one looks at it today.

Institutions, asthma, eczema, guilt, loneliness: none of this had subdued Zelda's supernatural energy. She had always been able to call upon it, whether for swimming, dancing, or writing. Her routine at the hospital in North Carolina was a Spartan one of hiking, calisthenics, abstemious diet, and promotion of modesty and nunlike submission by the absence of mirrors and cosmetics. Zelda stayed in this odd place, endured it all, for years, always being reminded of her "limitations" and "permanent damage." She died there and left in addition to her "legend" another memorial to her unkillable energy—an unfinished novel she intended to call *Caesar's Things.*

What are we to make of all this? Zelda's letters from the hospital are clear and courageous and searing to read. Certain schizophrenics make a strong appeal by the way in which the very limitations of their character remind harassed, responsible, intricately coping people of what they have lost—dreaminess, narrowness of concentration, inwardness, withdrawal. Also these sick persons create guilt of a mysterious kind, whether by their own wish or merely by the peculiarities of their often luminous fixity. The will to blame, to hold them to account, soon appears futile to those closest. Instead the mad entwine their relations in an unresolved, lingering, chafing connection, where guilt, exasperation and grief for the mysteries of life continue to choke. Perhaps the nearest feeling is the immensely suffering and baffling connection between those living and those slowly dying.

Fitzgerald's assumption of responsibility was woefully burdensome to him—and to his wife—but we feel, thinking of them together, that the burden and his bearing of it were at the very center of his moral being. It was his plot, his story, his symbol, image, destiny, obsession. Very few lives are of a piece in the way the Fitzgeralds' were; with them youth and middle age are linked not so much in the chain of growth as in the noose of cause and effect. Middle age is a bill left by youth, and the idea of bankruptcy is a recurring one in their thoughts. But the responsibility, the bearing of a burden, are important for Fitzgerald's idea of himself, perhaps because of his shame for his many weaknesses. He is never entirely free of the need to examine his case once more, never quite able to leave off weighing the cost to his best self, and, for that matter, his worst self. He is unimaginable to us without the weight of money to be made for others, memories to be faced in the middle of the night, the teasings of regret and the pleasures of loss.

Still, in taking the responsibility, however grumblingly and at whatever sacrifice, he was, unlike Zelda, able to find in it an action, a self-definition. A burden accepted is both a hump on your back and a star in your crown. To have disappeared, quit, even to have diminished his immense involvement would have left Fitzgerald with an unendurable emptiness and a feeling of masculine failure. For he not only worked in Hollywood and wrote for *The Saturday Evening Post* to support his wife and daughter, but he kept, week after week, month after month, this relentlessly punishing involvement of letters, arrangements, advice, complaints, nostalgia, new hope, new despair. (Hemingway, for instance, seems to have put aside his wives like last year's tweed jacket. He is not even able to say why he left the beautiful Hadley and his charming son, Bumby. He speaks only, in that careless way he and the Fitzgerald generation share, of "new people" and in some way the never explained temptations to forgetfulness provided by "the rich.")

The picture of Zelda we get from her letters is a disturbing one. The marriage was a misfortune, for they were prodigal partners, like a business marked for collapse because of the ghostly, paralyzing similarities of their natures. They enjoyed their exaggerations and follies when life worked; otherwise their compatibility was a disaster. Each needed just what the other lacked. Zelda was, for all her beauty and daring, hiding a deep sense of personal ambition, a feeling that there was something unique and possible inside her if only she could get at it, use it. Her energy and discipline never came to much. There was nothing she had mastered at quite the right time in her life, and perhaps it was, in the end, her suffering and madness, her breakdowns that frightened her finally into seeking some sort of health through these frantic artistic efforts.

Naturally, the brilliance could not flower. The efforts to live, be reborn, to be free, were at war with her nature and the twisted love that burned out both of these lives. Zelda's talents were in no way comparable to Fitzgerald's. Does this make a difference? Is it to the point? Art was the religion of the 1920s, and thus there were many women married to the tempestuous gods of the period, women called to share the thunder and lightning. Zelda's case was special. She too was anarchic, inspired, brilliant, unsteady, very much in her own way like the gods of the arts, like the spoiled, gifted, and famous all around her. In her, alas, the madness was real rather than an indulgence.

It is sad that her wish to learn, to struggle up to a higher skill and seriousness only seemed a threat to others. Her ways of trying to get well were always strenuous and they seemed to others merely an additional illness, or a deeper falling. What other ways than writing, dancing, or painting were open to her? In any case, failure in these hopes is ordinary and no dishonor lies in the effort. If she had not been married to Fitzgerald her "ambition" would not have presented itself as a "competition." Perhaps the result would have been the same; it would have been looked at differently, however.

Living as a sort of twin, as husband and wife or brother and sister, is a way of survival. In the case of artists these intense relations are curiously ambivalent, undefined collaborations—the two share in perceptions, temperament, in the struggle for creation, for the powers descending downward from art, for reputation, achievement, stability, for their own uniqueness—that especially. Still, only one of the twins is real as an artist, as a person with a special claim upon the world, upon the indulgence of society. Many writers seem to long for these trembling, gifted, outstanding handmaidens, for they are aware that the prosaic, the withdrawn, the demanding, are terrible daily deterrents to art and that the presence of an intelligent, sympathetic, clever sensibility, always at hand, always bright and somehow creative, is a source, even a source of material. With Zelda the *collaboration* was frenetic, almost a matter of essential being, of sharing of vices, arrogance, indulgence, as well as a central conception of themselves and their beautiful destructiveness as the core of Fitzgerald's fictional idea. And, of course, Zelda was always an enormous problem to a man beset with problems.

In spite of the glaring differences, she can bring to mind the exalted twinness of Dorothy and William Wordsworth and the sadness that always stands there, threatening, at the end of a life lived so intensely and with such disturbing self-consciousness. Mrs. Milford's book about Zelda Fitzgerald has in it what one might speak of as considerable "woman interest." A few years back the interest lay in the tragic grandeur and glamour of her love story. Now I should think it rests entirely in the heroism of her efforts and the bitterness of her defeats. She was flawed and rich with liability, but we suddenly find ourselves discontent and more than a little resentful that this strange, valuable girl from Montgomery, Alabama, had to endure unnecessary rebuffs and discouragements—in a life where so much suffering was foreordained and beyond repair.

In the end we feel about Zelda Fitzgerald just what De Quincey felt for Dorothy Wordsworth: "respectful pity."

Sylvia Plath

In SYLVIA PLATH'S work and in her life the elements of pathology are so deeply rooted and so little resisted that one is disinclined to hope for general principles, sure origins, applications, or lessons. Her fate and her themes are hardly separate and both are singularly terrible. Her work is brutal, like the smash of a fist; and sometimes it is also mean in its feeling. Literary comparisons are possible, echoes vibrate occasionally, but to whom can she be compared in spirit, in content, in temperament?

Certain frames for her destructiveness have been suggested by critics. Perhaps being born a woman is part of the exceptional rasp of her nature, a woman whose stack of duties was laid over the ground of genius, ambition, and grave mental instability. Or is it the 1950s, when she was going to college, growing up—is there something of that here? Perhaps; but I feel in her a special lack of national and local roots, feel it particularly in her poetry, and this I would trace to her foreign ancestors on both sides. They were given and she accepted them as a burden, not as a gift; but there they were, somehow cutting her off from what they weren't. Her father died when she was eight years old and this was serious, central. Yet this most interesting part of her history is so scorched by resentment and bitterness that it is only the special high burn of the bitterness that allows us to imagine it as a cutoff love.

For all the drama of her biography, there is a peculiar remoteness about Sylvia Plath. A destiny of such violent self-definition does not always bring the real person nearer; it tends, rather, to invite iconography, to freeze our assumptions and responses. She is spoken of as a "legend" or a "myth"—but what does that mean? Sylvia Plath was a luminous talent, self-destroyed at the age of thirty, likely to remain, it seems, one of the most interesting poets in American literature. As an *event* she stands with Hart Crane, Scott Fitzgerald, and Poe rather than with Emily Dickinson, Marianne Moore, or Elizabeth Bishop.

The outlines of her nature are odd, especially in her defiant and extensive capabilities, her sense of mastery, the craft and preparation she almost humbly and certainly industriously acquired as the foundation for an overwhelming ambition. She was born in Winthrop, Massachusetts. Her mother's parents were Austrian; her father was a German, born in Poland. He was a professor of biology, a specialist, among other interests, in bee-raising. (The ambiguous danger and sweetness of the beehive—totemic, emblematic for the daughter.) Her father died and the family moved to Wellesley, Massachusetts, to live with their grandparents. The mother became a teacher and the daughter went to public schools and later to Smith College. Sylvia Plath was a thorough success as a student and apparently was driven to try to master everything life offered—study, cooking, horseback riding, writing, being a mother, housekeeping. There seemed to have been in her character no empty patch or seam left for the slump, the incapacity, the refusal.

An early dramatic death gives one, in a literary sense, a real life, a throbbing biography. People discovered they had known a vehement, disturbing genius in their school days;

mere propinquity became a challenge, and the brief life has been the subject for memories of no special usefulness. Sylvia Plath does not come closer, shine more clearly. Poems have followed her poems, making their statements and to most of these her own harsh eloquence is the proper rebuke. We do not by any means have all of her letters, and the ones she must have written during the last year haunt the mind—that is, if she had the dependent, needy relationship that can make a letter an action, a true telling of feeling. The letters—at least the excerpts we have seen thus far—tend to be minimal, flat, suppressed, impersonal, rather more an instance of her lack of genuine closeness to the recipient than of any wish to reveal herself. A. Alvarez in *The Savage God* has done the greatest credit to the live person as he knew her. He is restrained, deeply knowledgeable about Sylvia Plath's poetry, and moved by the sufferings of her last days and the moment of suicide.

Sylvia Plath went on a Fulbright to Cambridge University. She met and later married the distinguished poet Ted Hughes, and after a year or so back in America they returned to live in England. Her first book of poems, *The Colossus,* was published in 1960, the same year her daughter Frieda was born. In 1962 her son Nicholas was born—and then life began to be hard and disturbing, except that she was able to write the poems later issued under the title *Crossing the Water.* She was separated from her husband, came back to London with two small children, tried to live and work and survive alone in a bare flat during one of the coldest years in over a century. *The Bell Jar* was published under a pseudonym just before she died, in February 1963.

In the last freezing months of her life she was visited, like some waiting stigmatist, by an almost hallucinating creativity—the astonishing poems in *Ariel* and in a later volume called *Winter Trees.*

The creative visitation was not from heaven, but from the

hell of rage. Yet so powerful is the art that one feels an unsettling elation as one reads the lacerating lines. The poems are about death, rage, hatred, blood, wounds, cuts, deformities, suicide attempts, stings, fevers, operations— there is no question of coming to terms with them. There is no consolation in our experience of the poems but they are alive, filled with hurt, excitement; a grinding, grating joy in the perfection of the descriptive language overcomes hesitations of the spirit.

There are also poems about children, her own, who were intensely loved. And yet "child" and "baby" as mere words are often attached to images of pain and death. Many of the poems are *tirades,* voiced at such a pitch of eloquence and passion they take your breath away. She, the poet, is frighteningly there all the time. Orestes rages, but Aeschylus lives to be almost seventy. Sylvia Plath, however, is both heroine and author; when the curtain goes down, it is her own dead body there on the stage, sacrificed to her plot.

She has the rarity of being, in her work at least, never a "nice person." There is nothing of mystical and schizophrenic vagueness about her. No dreamy loss of connection, no manic slackness, impatience, and lack of poetic judgment. She is, instead, all strength, ego, drive, endurance—and yet madly concentrated somehow, perplexing. Disgust is very strong in her nature, but she faces things with a classical fierceness and never loses dignity. That is why her vision is more powerful and more pure than the loose abandon of other poets of her period.

She is capable of anything—that we know. Alvarez reminds us how typical of her nature is the scene in *The Bell Jar* in which she dashes down a ski slope without knowing how to ski; he remembers her reckless way with horses, and tells of a deliberate smashing of her own car in a suicidal burst before the final one.

It is not recklessness that makes Sylvia Plath so forbidding, but destructiveness toward herself and others. Her mother thought *The Bell Jar* represented "the basest ingratitude" and we can only wonder at her innocence in expecting anything else. For the girl in the novel, a true account of events so far as we know, the ego is disintegrating and the stifling self-enclosure is so extreme that only death—and after that fails, shock treatment—can bring any kind of relief. Persons suffering in this way simply do not have room in their heads for the anguish of others—and later many seem to survive their own torments only by an erasing detachment. But even in recollection—and *The Bell Jar* was written a decade after the happenings—Sylvia Plath does not ask the cost.

There is a taint of paranoia in her novel and also in her poetry. The person who comes through is merciless and threatening, locked in violent images. If she does not, as so many have noticed, seem to feel pity for herself, neither is she moved to self-criticism or even self-analysis. It is a sour world, a drifting, humid air of vengeance. *The Bell Jar* seems to be a realistic account of her suicide attempt during the summer before her senior year at Smith. But the novel is about madness as well, and that separates it from the poems. Death, in the poetry, is an action, a possibility, a gesture, complete in itself, unmotivated, unexamined.

The Bell Jar opens with the line, "It was a queer, sultry summer, the summer they electrocuted the Rosenbergs." The Rosenbergs are in no way a part of the story and their mention is the work of an intelligence, wondering if the sufferings of a solitary self can have general significance. Also with her uncanny recognition of connections of all kinds— sound, sensation—and her poetic ordering of material, the electrocution of the Rosenbergs and the shock treatment at the end of the book have a metaphorical if not a realistic kinship. In the end the Rosenbergs just mean death to Sylvia

Plath. "I couldn't help wondering what it would be like, being burned alive, all along your nerves."

After a summer in New York, the girl goes back to Massachusetts and madness begins to close in on her. "I hadn't slept for twenty-one nights. I thought the most beautiful thing in the world must be shadow, the million moving shapes and cul de sacs of shadow. There was shadow in bureau drawers and closets and suitcases, and shadows under houses and trees and stones, and shadow at the back of people's eyes and smiles, and shadow, miles and miles of it, on the night side of the earth."

Committing suicide is desperation, demand for relief, but I don't see how we can ignore the way in which it is edged with pleasure and triumph in Sylvia Plath's work. In *The Bell Jar* she thinks of slashing her wrists in the tub and imagines the water "gaudy as poppies"—an image like those in her late poems. When she is unable to do the act, she still wants to "spill a little blood" for practice. "Then I felt a small, deep thrill, and a bright seam of red welled up at the lip of the slash. The blood gathered darkly, like fruit, and rolled down my ankle into the cup of my black patent leather shoe." These passages, and others much more brilliant in her poems, show a mind in a state of sensual distortion, seeking pain as much as death, contemplating with grisly lucidity the mutilation of the soul and the flesh. In "Daddy,"

> Every woman adores a Fascist,
> The boot in the face, the brute
> Brute heart of a brute like you.

With Sylvia Plath the submission to, the pursuit of pain are active, violent, *serious,* not at all in a Swinburnian mood of spankings and teasing degradation. Always, behind every mood, there is rage—for what reason we do not know, not even in the novel where the scene is open and explicit. In some poems the rage is directed blankly at her father, in others more obliquely, but with intensity, at her husband.

The actual suicide she attempted, and from which she was rescued only by great luck and accident, is very distressing in its details. The girl goes down into a cold, damp, cob-webbed corner of a cellar. There she hides herself behind an old log and takes fifty sleeping pills. The sense of downness, darkness, dankness, of unbearable rot and chill is savored for its ugliness and hurt. "They had to call and call / And pick the worms off me like sticky pearls" ("Lady Lazarus").

In real life there was a police search, newspaper headlines, empty pill bottle discovered; it was dramatic, unforgettable. Sylvia Plath was found, sent to the hospital, had shock treatment, and "the bell jar" in which she had been suffocating was finally lifted. The novel is not equal to the poems, but it is free of gross defects and embarrassments. The ultimate effort was not made, perhaps, but it is limited more in its intentions than in the rendering. The book has an interestingly cold, unfriendly humor. We sympathize with the heroine because of her drudging facing of it all and because of her suffering. The suffering is described more or less empirically, as if it were a natural thing, and the pity flows over you partly because she herself is so hard and glassy about her life.

This autobiographical work is written in a bare, rather collegiate 1950s style, and yet the attitude, the distance, and bitter carelessness are colored by a deep mood of affectlessness. The pleasures and sentiments of youth—wanting to be invited to the Yale prom, losing your virginity—are rather unreal in a scenario of disintegration, anger, and a perverse love of the horrible. The seduction of Esther Greenwood, as the heroine is called, is memorably grotesque and somehow bleakly suitable. The act led to a dangerous, lengthy, very unusual hemorrhaging. The blood—an obsession with the author—flows so plentifully that the girl is forced to seek medical help. She rather grimly pursues the young man with demands that he pay the doctor's bill, as if in some measure to get revenge for an action she herself cooperated with in the interest of experience.

The atrocious themes, the self-enclosure, the pain, blood, fury, infatuation with the hideous—all of that is in *The Bell Jar.* But, in a sense, softly, hesitantly. The poems in *Ariel* are much more violent. Indeed, the celebrated poem "Daddy" is as mean a portrait as one can find in literature.

Suicides are frequent enough, but the love of death, the teasing joy of it are rarely felt. Hart Crane, Virginia Woolf, many others, committed suicide. Some believe even Sappho threw herself from a rock into the sea. We think of these self-destructive actions as more or less sudden or as the culmination of an unbearable depression, one that brings with it a feeling of unworthiness and hopelessness, a despair that cannot imagine recovery.

Some of the journals Virginia Woolf wrote during the days before her death have in them the glittering contempt of a Sylvia Plath poem such as "Lesbos."

> Viciousness in the kitchen!
> The potatoes hiss.
> It is all Hollywood, windowless.

It goes on:

> You have stuck her kittens outside your window
> In a sort of cement well
> Where they crap and puke and cry and she can't hear.

This poem was written in the last weeks of Sylvia Plath's life and I have no clue as to whether or not it was an actual scene.

The excessive violence of the language, remarkable as it is, seems to come from a mind speeding along madly and yet commanding an uncanny control of language, sound, rhythm, and metaphor that is the very opposite of madness.

In the entry of Virginia Woolf's diary there is a similar impatience. "They were powdering and painting, these common little tarts . . . Then at Fuller's. A fat, smart woman in red hunting cap, pearls, check skirt, consuming rich cakes. Her shabby dependant also stuffing. . . . Where does the money come from to feed these fat white slugs?"

Anger and contempt. And yet, when the day comes for Virginia Woolf, the pain of the illness bears down on her and she feels only apology, gratitude, and depression. Her letter to her husband reads, "Dearest, I feel certain that I am going mad again. I feel we can't go through another of those terrible times. . . . I can't fight any longer. I know I am spoiling your life, that without me you could work." She weighted her skirts and managed to drown in the river.

With Sylvia Plath suicide is a performance. "Lady Lazarus" describes it with a raging, confident pride. There is no apology or fearfulness. Suicide is an assertion of power, of the strength—not the weakness—of the personality. She is no poor animal sneaking away, giving up; instead she is strong, threatening, dangerous.

> I have done it again.
> One year in every ten
> I manage it—
>
>   "Lady Lazarus"

Sometimes the performance is a reposeful one, as in "Edge":

> The woman is perfected.
> Her dead

> Body wears the smile of accomplishment,
> The illusion of a Greek necessity

Occasionally, as in the ending of "Last Words," domesticity and annihilation are mixed together:

> When the soles of my feet grow cold,
> The blue eye of my turquoise will comfort me.
> Let me have my copper cooking pots, let my rouge pots
> Bloom about me like night flowers, with a good smell.
> They will roll me up in bandages, they will store my heart
> Under my feet in a neat parcel. . . .

Sylvia Plath's preoccupation with the body at the moment of death reminds me of Mishima, although her concern is not to be "fit" as his apparently was, but simply to have the sensation of the corpse. With both of these suicides the action is asserted as a value, a definition, a pure leap. It is even sometimes thought of as beautiful, "pure and clean as the cry of a baby."

The circumstances of her suicide in London, the expectation that a girl would be coming in early to help with the children, the knowledge that the man in the flat below awakened early, the note with the doctor's name and phone number: these facts lead Alvarez to speculate that Sylvia Plath didn't *entirely* want to kill herself. She *risked* death—and lost.

Suicide, in that view, is thought of as a cry for help, one that cannot be uttered in the usual ways. The sheer fact of it was a tragic culmination, and yet it is not the death but the obsessions with it that are her inexplicable subject matter. Torture, mutilation, destruction are offered as interesting in themselves, without any suggestions that they are a "problem." Mishima tried to decorate his death with ideas of national policy which were, of course, ridiculous fantasies. Sylvia Plath always seems to be describing her self-destruction as an exhilarating act of contempt.

Perhaps it is important to remember that the poems are about suicide rather than about death as the waiting denouement of every life. The oddity of this is almost inexhaustible and the poems break with the universal theme of the passage of time, decay of the body, union with God, whatever death in the English poetic tradition has attached itself to. The idea of killing oneself, the sensuality of it, the drama of it, the prevision, based on other attempts, cannot fail to be a distortion, a decadence. The death wish, that limping, hanging-back companion to life, is, if it exists, an instinctual compliment to the vast and intricate efforts to survive. It is not one with a steady compulsion to jump, slit one's throat, swallow pills, turn on the gas.

The suicides are, then, a group apart, technicians, planners, plotters. Anne Sexton shares the wish, and her prose and poem about Sylvia Plath's death are strange, jaunty, casual and rather rapid, as if one were telling an anecdote in fear of interruption. She speaks of the two of them as "death-mongers," and tells with great excitement of the way they talked "their deaths in the Ritz Bar in Boston." Feel the air, imagine the scene, she says, "We talked about death with a burned-up intensity, both of us drawn to it like moths to an electric light bulb. Sucking on it!" The gaiety is profoundly saddening, the glittering eye frightens us. Anne Sexton tries, in a poem, to explain the peculiar concern for craft that dominates the suicide's imagination:

> Like carpenters they want to know which tools.
> They never ask why build.

Suicide is only one of the distressing themes in Sylvia Plath's work. There is fascination with hurt and damage and

fury; she is a bluntly acute and rather heartless observer.
There is a blind man at the table on a ship, feeling for his
food. "His fingers had the noses of weasels. I couldn't stop
looking." The bright reds of poppies and tulips become
bloody and threatening. Gifts are not easily accepted. Slashing a finger in the kitchen is the occasion for "Cut," with its
transfixed accuracy.

> What a thrill—
> My thumb instead of an onion.
> The top quite gone
> Except for a sort of hinge
>
> Of skin,
> A flap like a hat,
> Dead white.
> Then that red plush.

A bruise is, in like manner, painted in "Contusion."

> Colour floods to the spot, dull purple.
> The rest of the body is all washed out.
> The colour of pearl.

Is the poem "Daddy" to be accepted as a kind of exor-
cism, a wild dramatic monologue of abuse screamed at a
lost love?

> You do not do, you do not do
> Any more, black shoe
> In which I have lived like a foot
> For thirty years, poor and white,
> Barely daring to breathe or Achoo.

Her father died of a long illness, but there is no pity for *his*
lost life. Instead he is not the dead one; he is the murderer:

An engine, an engine
Chuffing me off like a Jew
A Jew to Dachau, Auschwitz, Belsen.
I began to talk like a Jew.
I think I may well be a Jew.

The association of her own pain with that of the Jews in Europe has been named very well by George Steiner, "a subtle larceny." The father did not kill anyone and "the fat black heart" is really her own. How is it possible to grieve for more than twenty years for one as evil and brutal as she asserts her father to have been? On the grounds of psychology every opposite can be made to fall neatly into place— that jagged, oddly shaped piece is truly part of a natural landscape if only you can find the spot where its cutting corners slip into the blue sky. The acrimonious family—yes, any contrary can turn up there, *logically* as it were. But even strangers, the town, are brought into the punishment of her father and this is somehow the most biting and ungenerous thought of all:

There's a stake in your fat black heart
And the villagers never liked you.
They are dancing and stamping on you.
They always knew it was you.
Daddy, daddy, you bastard, I'm through.

She insists that she is the victim—poor and white, a Jew, with a pretty red heart. But she is a dangerous and vindictive casualty: "Herr God, Herr Lucifer / Beware / Beware." "Daddy," with its hypnotic rhythms, its shameful harshness, is one of Sylvia Plath's most popular and known works. You cannot read it without shivering. It is done, completed, perfected. All the hatred in our own hearts finds its evil unforgiving music there—the Queen of the Night.

Love for her children, what about that? Isn't it mitigating? There is warmth and even joy. The boy and girl are "two roses," a child's smile is "found money," children are "the one solid the spaces lean on," the baby is a "high-riser, my little loaf." But children also appear in the images of destruction. In "Edge" the woman who is perfected by death has her dead children with her.

She has folded

Them back into her body as petals
Of a rose close when the garden

Stiffens and odours bleed
From the sweet, deep throats of the night flower.

A child's smile is a "hook." There is a poem about the deformities occasioned by thalidomide. In "Death & Co.":

He tells me how sweet
The babies look in their hospital
Icebox, a simple

Frill at the neck,
Then the flutings of their Ionian
Death gowns,
Then two little feet.

What can we make of a poet so ambitious and vengeful, so brilliant and yet so willfully vulnerable? How can we judge such a sense of personal betrayal, such rage, and such deformed passions? Her work is overwhelming; it is quite literally irresistible. The daring, the skill, the severity. It shocks and thrills. She called—in a typically awful phrase—her last burst of poetry "the blood jet."

When the time came she had earned it by all those earlier

poems, slowly, carefully written, by that long ambition, burning, waiting, learning, by her A's, her Phi Beta Kappa, her driven perfectionism, her arrogance, her madness controlled to just the right degree. The loneliness which Alvarez so compellingly preserves for us, the freezing flat—without curtains—the icy early mornings, furiously writing before the children cried and before the "glassy music" of the milkman, her husband off with someone else—there we have a "modern instance" if there ever was one.

It is not a question in these last weeks of the conflict in a woman's life between the claims of the feminine and the agonized work of art. Every artist is either a man or a woman and the struggle is pretty much the same for both. All art that is not communal is, so to speak, made at home. Sylvia Plath was furious. Alvarez writes:

> I suspect that finding herself alone again now, however temporarily and voluntarily, all the anguish she had experienced at her father's death was reactivated: despite herself, she felt abandoned, injured, enraged and bereaved as purely and defenselessly as she had as a child twenty years before.

The sense of betrayal, even of hatred, did not leave her weak and complaining so much as determined and ambitious. Ambitious rage is all over *Ariel* and in the poems written at the same time and published in *Winter Trees*. "The Applicant" is a very bitter poem about the woman's part in marriage. In "For a Fatherless Son" she speaks to the child about the absence of the father that will gradually grow in the child's consciousness like a tree:

> A death tree, color gone, an Australian gum tree—
> Balding, gelded by lightning—an illusion,
> And a sky like a pig's backside, an utter lack of attention.

And that is what her own life was like at the end—the husband and father's "utter lack of attention."

In the explosive energy of her last months I see a determination to "win." Indeed I feel, from the evidence of her work, that it is sentimental to keep insisting that the birth of her children unlocked her poetic powers. Why should that be? The birth of children opens up the energy for taking care of them and for loving them. The common observation that one must be prepared to put off other work for a few years is strongly founded. Of course, it is foolish to generalize and it is the work itself, its hard competitiveness that glare out at every turn. When she died she was alone, exhausted from writing, miserable—but triumphant too, achieved, defined and defiant.

The suicide of a young woman with the highest gifts is inevitably a circumstance of the most moving and dramatic sort. We cannot truly separate the work from the fascination and horror of the death. It is a fact that the poems in *Ariel* were read, while Sylvia Plath was alive, with full self-control and detachment by editors, who then rejected many that have since become important additions to our literature. In the end this does not strike me as more than an astonishment and it is certain the poems would have been published. Everything, everything is published, and no matter that the claim upon our attention is more often than not unfathomable. What is more teasing to the mind and the imagination is how the poems of a dramatic suicide would read to us if the poet had held on to life, given interviews, public readings, finished a second novel, more poems.

It is interesting to make the effort to read Sylvia Plath's poems as if she were still alive. They are just as brilliant, just as much creations of genius, but they are obscured and altered. Blood, reds, the threats do not impress themselves so painfully upon us. "Cold blanks approach us:/They move in a hurry." What is that? we wonder. Unhappiness, agitation, fear? "Edge" seems to be a Greek heroine, Medea perhaps, once more. "Last Words," a profoundly well-written poem:

> I do not want a plain box, I want a sarcophagus
> With tigery stripes, and a face on it
> Round as the moon, to stare up.

A beautiful poem in which, as the textbooks might say, the poet imagines her own death and is buried in a tomb, like an ancient Babylonian goddess of love. "The Detective," a prophetic poem about a death (or is it a murder?) that imagines us as we have become—detectives, putting the pieces together, working on the case. "Make notes," it says at the end.

Her poems have, read differently, the overcharged preoccupation with death and release found in religious poetry. For indeed she saw eternity the other night, also; she cries out "No end?" as Herbert does. But she was not religious; instead she is violently secular in her eternities, realistic about the life that slides from her side. Suicide was not a necessity to the passion and brilliance of the poems; nevertheless the act is a key, central to the overwhelming burst of achievement. She lived on her poetry during the last months of her life. Great she knew it to be; we feel that. It had to be *serious,* final. To imagine anyone's taking his life as a way of completing, fulfilling, explaining the highest work of that life may appear impudent, insulting to death. And yet is it more thoughtful to believe that love, debts, ill health, revenge are greater values to the human soul than creative, artistic powers? Artists have often been cruel to others for what they imagined to be advantages to their work. Cruelty to oneself, as the completion of creation, is far from unimaginable, especially to a spirit tempted throughout life to self-destruction.

If anything could have saved Sylvia Plath it would have been that she, in life, might have had the good fortune to know her own fulfillment, her hard, glittering achievement. In *The Review,* Douglas Dunn wrote about her: "Sylvia Plath was one of the most remarkable talents in any art of the decade, if not of the century." She has won the green cloth—no writer ever wanted it more. Or it would be more careful to say that she *earned* the green cloth and along with the first determination to be preeminent as a poet there came money and power, all by her own efforts. But it came too late, of course, and lesser spirits usurped the ground, began the sentimentalization of her own ungenerous nature and unrelenting anger.

Beyond the mesmerizing rhythms and sounds, the flow of brilliant, unforgettable images, the intensity—what does she say to her readers? Is it simple admiration for the daring, for going the whole way? To her fascination with death and pain she brings a sense of combat and brute force new in women writers. She is vulnerable, yes, to father and husband, but that is not the end of it at all. I myself do not think her work comes out of the cold war, the extermination camps, or the anxious doldrums of the Eisenhower years. If anything, she seems to have jumped ahead of her dates and to have more in common with the years we have just gone through. Her lack of conventional sentiment, her destructive contempt for her family, the failings in her marriage, the drifting, rootless rage, the peculiar homelessness, the fascination with sensation and the drug of death, the determination to try everything, knowing it would not really stop the suffering—no one went as far as she did in this.

There is nothing of the social revolutionary in her, but she is whirling about in the center of an overcharged, splitting air and she especially understands everything destructive and negative. What she did not share with the youth of the present is her intense and perfect artistry, her belief in it. That religion she seemed to have got from some old Prussian root memory of hard work, rigor, self-command. She is a stranger, an alien. In spite of her sea imagery—and it is not particularly local but rather psychological—she is hard to connect with Massachusetts and New England. There is nothing Yankee in her. So "crossing the water" was easy— she was as alien to nostalgia and sentiment as she was to the country itself. A basic and fundamental displacement played its part.

Sylvia Plath has extraordinary descriptive powers; it is a correctness and accuracy that combine the look of things with their fearsome powers of menace. It is not close to the magnifying-glass descriptions in Marianne Moore and Elizabeth Bishop, that sense these two writers have of undertaking a sort of decoding, startling in the newness of what is seen. When Elizabeth Bishop writes that the "donkey brays like a pump gone dry," this is a perfectly recognizable and immensely gratifying gift of the sort we often get also in Sylvia Plath. But the detail in Elizabeth Bishop's "The Fish" is of another kind:

> I looked into his eyes
> which were far larger than mine
> but shallower, and yellowed,
> the irises backed and packed
> with tarnished tinfoil
> seen through the lenses
> of old scratched isinglass.

Marianne Moore's abstruse, peering investigations, her shining, gleaming mirror reflect—more than anything else— words. For instance, "Smooth Gnarled Crepe Myrtle" and its flowing compounds:"

> A brass-green bird with grass-
> green throat smooth as a nut springs from

twig to twig askew, copying the
Chinese flower piece—business-like atom
in the stiff-leafed tree's blue-
pink dregs—of wine pyramids
of mathematic
circularity; one of a
pair.

In Marianne Moore and Elizabeth Bishop we are never far away from the comic spirit, from tolerance and wisdom—qualities alien to the angry illuminations of *Ariel*. But the tradition is also strong in Sylvia Plath—and taste, too, in the sense of craft utterly conquered and absorbed. Precision interests her, and she is immensely learned like the other two poets, never wishing to be a "natural" in any sense. She has also the power of the visual, part of the preference for precision over rhetoric. Perhaps this greed for particulars is the true mark of the poetry of women in our time. In the end, what is overwhelming, new, original, in Sylvia Plath is the burning singularity of temperament, the exigent spirit clothed but not calmed by the purest understanding of the English poetic tradition.

Long after I had been reading her work I came across the recording of some of her poems she made in England not long before she died. I have never before learned anything from a poetry reading, unless the clothes, the beard, the girls, the poor or good condition of the poet can be considered a kind of knowledge. But I was taken aback by Sylvia Plath's reading. It was not anything like I could have imagined. Not a trace of the modest, retreating, humorous Worcester, Massachusetts, of Elizabeth Bishop; nothing of the swallowed plain Pennsylvania of Marianne Moore. Instead these bitter poems—"Daddy," "Lady Lazarus," "The Applicant," "Fever 103"—were "beautifully" read, projected in full-throated, plump, diction-perfect, Englishy, mesmerizing cadences, all round and rapid, and paced and spaced. Poor recessive Massachusetts had been erased. "I have done it again!" Clearly, perfectly, staring you down. She seemed to be standing at a banquet like Timon, crying, "Uncover, dogs, and lap!"

It is a tragic story, completely original and unexpected in its scenes and its themes. Ted Hughes, her husband, has a poem about wives:

> Their brief
> Goes straight up to heaven and nothing more is heard of it.

That was not true of Sylvia Plath, and since we now have no choice perhaps there is no need to weigh and to wonder whether her awful black brief was worth it.

Bloomsbury and
Virginia Woolf

BLOOMSBURY is, just now, like one of those ponds on a private estate from which all of the trout have been scooped out for the season. It is not a natural place for fish, but rather a water stocked for the fisherman so that he may not cast his line in vain. It is a catered pastoral, and lively, thoroughbred trout rise to the fly with a special leaping grace and style. But it wearies as an idea, a design, a gathering, and one would like to have each speckled specimen alone, singular. The period, the letters, the houses, the love affairs, the blood lines: these are private anecdotes one is happy enough to meet once or twice but not again and again.

Certain peripheral names scratch the mind. To see the word "Ottoline" on a page, in a letter, gives me the sense of continual defeat, as if I had gone to a party and found an enemy attending the bar. We, foreigners, will never take her in, although it seems we must. She is everywhere, but what is to be made of her? She engages them, Englishmen, endlessly and the rest of us not at all. Her invitations, her gifts, her houses, her costumes—the best minds of a generation (or two) rocked back and forth, pro and con, up and down over the quality and meaning of these. For years I thought Garsington, Lady Ottoline's house, was a town name, a resort clever people were always going to or making a point of not going to. Hedonism is only a habit and the brightness of its practices fades with the dawn.

"What a fool Clive Bell is!" Lawrence says in one of his letters. Is that true, just? The one certain thing is that he is Virginia Woolf's brother-in-law, husband of Vanessa, father of Quentin Bell, the author of the important *Virginia Woolf: A Biography.*

The worst thing before the present exhaustion of Virginia Woolf was the draining of Lytton Strachey. This is a very overblown affair, right down to his friend Carrington, who committed suicide forty years ago—an unreclaimable figure, fluid, arrested, charming, very much a girl of the period, with the typical Bloomsbury orderly profligacy and passionate coldness. Her marriage and her love affairs are held in the mind for a day or so after hard study, but they soon drift away to the Carrington haunt. Ralph Partridge, yes: he turns up again at the Hogarth Press.

In a recent *New Statesman,* there was a moving and, to me, instructive portrait by V.S. Pritchett of the painter Mark Gertler, another Bloomsbury figure and another Bloomsbury current biography. Gertler grips your feelings immediately because of the sufferings he has passed and because of their roots in the fatalities and miseries of social history—for his link with the universal, for a drama in which the world plays a part. In him are absent all the proprieties of education, circumstance, and style that marked the Bloomsbury friend-ships. Gertler was Jewish, poor, contracted tuberculosis from the London slums; his marriage failed, his children suffered illnesses; he was eccentric, melancholy, one of those persons who will, no matter what successes briefly touch them, know lingering failure. "Nazism and anti-Semitism in Germany were the last straw" and he committed suicide.

Idly, even wistfully, pursuing the beaded cross references of this study, I looked him up in the index of *Carrington.*

And there indeed lay the bones of the tormented man: "Gertler, Mark: . . . C. has sexual relations with, 50–51, 53, 68–69; C.'s break with, 63–67. . . ."

Lytton Strachey, brilliant, master of a rich, balanced popular style, had about him an arrogance that did not exclude the possibilities of loyalty, friendship, and love for those persons he could tolerate. He is witty, eccentric, curious, learned, and outrageous, a perfect Bloomsbury blending of homosexuality and donnish talents, true ones. He is likely to switch from the question of conscription in World War I to "the really interesting question" of a paper he read at the meeting of the Apostles group at Cambridge in 1911.

The really interesting question concerns me—the particular me— and Alexis—the particular (but not too particular) Alexis. It concerns the particular kiss I gave him on a particular day, in the sun, with the hollyhocks all round, and the lawn, and some confused people out of sight in the distance—don't you see it all? Oh, but it is just the *all* that you don't see.

Alexis, whom one and perhaps Strachey himself, had thought of as a golden-haired youth, is soon admitted to be dull, ugly, nearly bald, and this bit of a reversal, this *reality,* the questioning of it, the bold, mannered embarrassment of it, occupied Strachey, and no doubt his conversation, as much as Queen Victoria or Florence Nightingale. The popularity of his writing is surprising—or, rather, it is surprising that he could wish to write in so successful and dramatic a way. His person, loved in his circle, was not very likely to take in ordinary humanity. He was too free in his eccentricities, too marked by his class and the wild peculiarities of his appearance and manners.

And what do we have in the end about Bloomsbury from the small score of personal anecdote relentlessly repeated? I am struck—in the memorials and essays by writers who were young and yet present when Virginia Woolf was alive—by the sameness of tone, the valuable little core of things each one held close. Still, this was it, the reality—and anything further or different would be a straining for novelty and perhaps, for the English, an irreverence, a violation of a genius and character altogether rare, high, and tortured.

Something is wrong. For myself I could never have imagined especially wishing to read Leonard Woolf's autobiography except for the accounts of Virginia Woolf's breakdowns and suicide—and these fall very short of what I might in a low moment have liked to have. There are many biographies, from all countries, like that of Leonard Woolf. He was a good man; he worked hard in a number of colorful settings; he knew many interesting people; he engaged in creditable actions and held decent opinions with tenacity. No matter, in the end Virginia Woolf's suicide letter was worth it all, although one would never have wanted to think this when the books were freshly coming out.

Then the force of Bloomsbury and "brightest things that are theirs" claimed the mind. The wood smoke, a life still courteous and unconventional, people handsome and malicious and serious and never boring—and as all of this swells and inflates there is reason for gratitude and pride in it. It is an English matter. Americans cannot quite get it straight except for the grand, isolated singularities like Virginia Woolf, fortunately a feminist, and E. M. Forster, fortunately the author of an international novel. Bertrand Russell cannot be brought under the umbrella of Bloomsbury, nor can Maynard Keynes, except in his homosexual youth. What is popular about Bloomsbury at the moment is its gay liberation, its serious high camp.

The sex life was truly alive. No Brook Farm or Brahmins or Concord Transcendentalists or Midwest alcoholics to deface the pursuit of pleasure, to stumble in the following of where she would go. True, Bloomsbury lacks the demonic. Think of all the years we waited for Forster's *Maurice,* a very interesting novel perfectly suited to publication at any time. It was what we might have known it would be: the suspense came from the withholding, the *retention,* as it were.

The "swapping" is interesting. This practice one had thought confined to certain earnest Americans in the smaller, more tedious cities, to those wives and husbands who had read sex manuals and radically wanted more of life even if it had to be, like pizza, brought in from around the corner —all of this was accomplished by Bloomsbury in the lightest, most spontaneous and good-natured manner. Vanessa Bell is a heroine. She is beautiful, interesting, free. She falls in love and lives with her husband, Clive Bell, and at other times with their friends, Roger Fry and Duncan Grant. Want of industry leaves the affairs without perfect clarity in my mind, but the drift of experience is striking.

Jealousy and possessiveness seem, from the books we have, not so much held in check as somehow never achieving vigorous birth in Bloomsbury. Even Bertrand Russell astonishes with his passionless copulations, his mastery of forgetfulness, his sliding in and out of relationships and marriages as if they were a pair of trousers. When Virginia Woolf "fell in love" it was not with some soft-eyed, sighing, brilliant feminist met in the British Museum, but with Vita Sackville-West, Harold Nicolson's wife, a woman "suitable" and civilized in the highest degree.

The two transcendent loyalties and fidelities were both angular and chaste. They are impressive and in many ways more of a glory to the ideal of personal relations than the other freely shifting associations. Carrington's love for Lytton Strachey, her sharing of his life for seventeen years, is a rare instance of a complicated need for a love between man and woman, without sex—a love that miraculously found its object. Carrington's devotion was so great that when Strachey died of cancer her own life seemed empty and not worth living and she committed suicide.

Leonard Woolf's endurance of Virginia's famous frigidity is, we must suppose after the fact, altogether to his credit. Their honeymoon did not bring the amelioration they had hoped for and it is incredibly innocent and moving to think of them discussing it with Vanessa. They wanted to know when she had first had an orgasm. She said she couldn't remember but she knew she had been "sympathetic" from the age of two. Vita Sackville-West said about Virginia, "She dislikes the possessiveness and love of domination in men. In fact she dislikes the quality of masculinity."

The arrangements of Bloomsbury, shored up by stout logs of self-regard, are insular in the extreme. One of the advantages of remaining on the upper deck is that the possibilities of jealousy, whining, threats, blackmail, outrage are comfortably diminished. And boredom and effort also. But the need for experience, for danger, for hurt, for *life*, actually for sex itself as a dramatic and mysterious engagement, is found in the homosexuals. Unfortunately those baffled youths, caught in the unique spidery embraces of Lytton Strachey, do not write letters or diaries—if they did it would likely be with criminal intention. (This sort of letter is perfectly composed by Forster in *Maurice:* "i waited both nights in the boathouse. I said the boathouse as the ladder is taken away and the woods is too damp to lie down. . . .") In the long run the boys have a deformed kind of style; virility is itself an aesthetic value.

Style matters. In Virginia Woolf's novels most of the characters are complicated men and women, creatures of intricate feeling, and they are seen more or less on their own terms, from the inside, profoundly, since this, the inside, was

the thing she valued. However, she does occasionally insert
a repellent person. In *Mrs. Dalloway* it is the envying, op-
pressive Miss Kilman, a shadow from the half-educated,
unattractive, resentful underclasses. She is the object of the
author's insolent loathing. Miss Kilman is not evil, she is
merely unappetizing. Her social and personal defects are
confronted in a peculiarly exasperated mood, without pity or
inhibition or the veiling of a mitigating causality. She is
externalized, politicized by her exclusion. Characters of this
sort are hated for their self-pity and for their yearning ignorance. They are people who know a little and may want to
know much. Yet they cannot learn deeply; some lacks of
birth or temperament prevent it.

Miss Kilman is poor, but she has her degree. The war has
displaced her as a teacher and she is hanging on by her
fingernails to a low-burning encounter with religion. Even
this has not come to her with a flush of glory, but rather like
a dispiriting brush with a flu germ. The awful woman eats
too much; she embarrasses us with her greed for the last pink
tea cake. Her green mackintosh is disgusting; "she perspires."

Remember Leonard Bast in Forster's *Howards End:* the
same heartless, *ill-mannered candor* on the part of the author.

He knew that he was poor, and would admit it: he would have
died sooner than confess any inferiority to the rich. . . . But he was
inferior to most rich people, there is not the least doubt of it. He
was not as courteous as the average rich man, nor as intelligent,
nor as healthy, nor as lovable.

The thing that is unforgivable to the authors is the way the
characters reach, in the manner of a car crashing into a wall,
a cultural impasse, a stopping. They cannot understand art;

they cannot discriminate. They never get it right. "But of a heritage that may expand gradually, he had no conception; he hoped to come to Culture suddenly, much as the Revivalist hopes to come to Jesus."

Henry James's seriously disturbing story "In the Cage" is a work written entirely out of a drastic condescension on the part of the author—and it is this, the wonder how far, how painfully he will push on, that holds us to these fascinating pages. Any triumph in this kind of writing is abstract; it is the author's mimicry of the wretched persons' handicaps. It is not satire. You cannot satirize an idiot; you can only do that if the idiot has, for instance, achieved the post of judge or come into a fortune. In *Mrs. Dalloway* the other loathed character is seen satirically because he is the proper object for the satiric mode. He is (son of a shopkeeper—and inevitably so, we must add) Sir William Bradshaw, an appallingly vulgar and shallow psychiatrist, carrying about with him his load of satiric character props, the main one being a pert lecture on "proportion" which he likes to deliver to madmen standing on the ledge of suicide.

In the James story the girl in the cage is a little telegraph operator. During the summer season the most stimulating messages are pushed under the wire for her to send off. Nicknames, codes, engagements made, engagements broken, the prodigality of "the 'much love's and the 'awful' regrets"; she, through their telegrams, inserts herself into their "struggles and secrets and love affairs and lies. . . . " Characters like the girl in the cage and Miss Kilman swing back and forth between a cow-eyed servility and the flames of a spasmodic, disastrous pride. And as if one character were not enough, James has in his story dialogues and confrontations between two, the other being a foolish widow who has struck up a kind of business looking after the flowers in the houses of the rich. The widow's folly is in imagining that the iron and stone of social barriers are really "the thinnest of partitions."

The girl in the cage and the widow of the flowers compete with each other in carefully tense and trembling dialogues:

> "Well, I see everyone at *my* place."
> "Everyone?"
> "Lots of swells. They flock. They live, you know, all round, and the place is filled with all the smart people, all the fast people, those whose names are in the papers. . . ."
> Mrs. Jordan took this in with complete intelligence. "Yes, and I dare say it's some of your people that I do."
> Her companion assented, but discriminated. "I doubt if you 'do' them as much as I! Their affairs, their appointments and arrangements, their little games and secrets and vices—those things all pass before me."
> ". . . Their vices? Have they got vices?"
> Our young critic even more overtly stared; ". . . Haven't you found *that* out?" The homes of luxury then hadn't so much to give. "I find out everything."
> Mrs. Jordan, at bottom a very meek person, was visibly struck. "I see. You do 'have' them."

There is something unscrupulous and sadistic in this rendering. One is not prepared to accept simply as writing that Mrs. Dalloway's disgust with Miss Kilman (perfectly convincing and novelistically suitable) should be so completely shared by Virginia Woolf. We don't know from whose point of view the telegraph operator and the flower-watcher are being so carefully exposed unless it is from that of the author. And who tells us that Leonard Bast cannot be as lovable as a rich man? These passages are strange, raw insertions, like uncontrollable bits of opinion coming from outside the fiction.

The reader does not necessarily go along with the author. It is recognized more or less unconsciously as the pages go by that we don't take it all in the way it is meant. Miss Kilman is a mess; but Virginia Woolf is "awful" to write "she perspires." It doesn't matter to us that she hates a woman like Miss Kilman; we'd rather not be told. Mrs. Dalloway, the character, is another matter; one of her limitations is lack of curiosity and another is a charming, almost hysterical attachment to surfaces. There are ways in which it is bad taste for authors to come down so heavily on the lacks of the luckless and deprived, to tell off these penniless souls as if they were Veneerings or Verdurins.

I wonder about the "morality" of certain marks of punctuation used by James in "In the Cage." When characters are seen from the outside, viewed solely in the glinting suspicions of a sensibility utterly foreign to their own, style tells us the author's prejudices and impatience, his hatreds, his limitations of feeling. *He* makes as many mistakes as his characters, shows a certain coarseness of perception, or a degree of meanness, or an inclination to self-love. The telegraph girl is allowed only the swiftest, lightest taps of personal identification. It is all down, down, the very bottom—sister, mother, all of them. In the midst of her upward longings, her rising misconnections, the girl pauses unexpectedly, in a clause, at the end of the most externally conceived, impudent Jamesian depiction of her—she pauses and "made up even for the most haunting of her worries, the rage at moments of not knowing how her mother did 'get it.' "

"Get it" is alcohol, gin probably. The down, down mother ("never rebounded any more at the bottom than on the way down") drinks. The shadow that falls across the brisk superficialities of the girl is one of real misery, torment, hopelessness. It must be so; it cannot be otherwise, even though nothing is made of it. We add the misery from our own experience or imagination to the reduced brief obliquities by which we were informed in the first place. To put "get it" in quotations is a moral failing; it pretends it is a mere colloqui-alism identified, or asks that we in our minds put some peculiar stress on it that will equal the accentual patterns in the author's mind, or wants to indicate an affectation on the girl's part—any of those things the mimicry of quotation marks may suggest. But this is wrong. "Get it" in this case is not on the level of Mrs. Jordan's "have" quoted above. Even a second of an impoverished mother's pursuit of gin cannot be put on the page in that way. It accomplishes only a stylistic diminishment of the possibility of pain, of real feeling.

Quentin Bell's *Virginia Woolf* is somewhat redundant for those of us who have been through Lytton Strachey, Carring-ton, and Leonard Woolf—just yesterday it seemed. But that is not Bell's fault; it is a mere contingency. He tells it all gracefully, having, one imagines, struggled hard to find his way between piety and indiscretion. Some have felt that Bell avoids unfairly the close examination of her work that we might expect from a biographer of a novelist. Yet how is that work to be written about? Exegesis about Virginia Woolf is a trap; the fictions are circular and the critic spins in a drum of tautology.

The novels are beautiful; the language is rich and pure, and you are always, with her, aware of genius, of gifts extraordi-nary and original. Our emotions are moved, at least some of our emotions are moved, often powerfully. And yet in a sense her novels aren't interesting. This is the paradox of her work, part of the risk of setting a goal in fiction, of having an idea about it, an abstract idea. Part of the risk also of the bravest and most daring insistence that she would make something new. It is common to speak of her novels as "poetic," and they are like poetry in their use of language, and also they have that quality so often found in "poetic" prose—that sense of being all chorus, beautiful, urgent, composed rhythmically, stressing theme in an image. All chorus and no plot, that is the danger of her wish, her vision. Part of her freedom, her arrogance was to do just this. She refuses the practical, the complete, doesn't believe in them. And what can we do but accept that choice?

What is the point of hinting that she might better have a little more of Arnold Bennett than she does? And what is the point of paraphrasing *The Waves,* of trying for your own circles of ebb and flow to compete with hers? I was immensely moved by this novel when I read it recently and yet I cannot think of anything to say about it except that it is wonderful. The people are not characters, there is no plot in the usual sense. What can you bring to bear: verisimilitude —to what? You can merely say over and over that it is very good, very beautiful, that when you were reading it you were happy.

One of the things that make *To the Lighthouse* interesting for the reader who is also a writer is that, in this case, one can bring things in from the outside. If Mr. and Mrs. Ramsay are in some way Virginia Woolf's mother and father, then you have Leslie Stephen as a character. And upstairs you have his *Hours in a Library, Studies of a Biographer,* the thin, green *George Eliot.* These are books I have used, but I have not learned greatly from them. Still, when Mr. Ramsay appears in his being as a writer, we are watching something real, immensely affecting—the poignancy of a long, hard literary life. "He wanted sympathy. He was a failure, he said. Mrs. Ramsay flashed her needles. Mr. Ramsay repeated, never taking his eyes from her face, that he was a failure."

Nostalgia is the emotion most deeply felt in Virginia Woolf's novels. They are family books. Husbands, wives, old lovers, youth, memories, death, the drift of life. "What is this terror? What is this ecstasy?" and "Against you I will fling myself, unvanquished and unyielding, O Death!" . . . *The waves broke on the shore.* Nostalgia is passive, the books are passive, requiems, unlike any other. Perhaps this is her melancholy.

The movement, the action, the stir of her life, were in her writing. The drama was a book finished, another undertaken. Her madness is in the writing at times, too, perhaps in the endless, stretching sense we have of life as a soliloquy.

"Life, how I have dreaded you," said Rhoda. "Oh, human beings, how I have hated you! How you have nudged, how you have interrupted, how hideous you have looked in Oxford Street, how squalid sitting opposite each other staring in the Tube! Now as I climb this mountain, from the top of which I shall see Africa, my mind is printed with brown-paper parcels and your faces."

Her husband, Leonard Woolf, speaks always of the need for rest. Does he mean restraint? Hard to believe such severe derangements subdued by rest. Their life was difficult and if Leonard Woolf sometimes seems too rigid and puritanical and orderly for her, who can doubt that it was for the best? Her achievement in the face of the hideous distractions of madness is miraculous. He suffered extravagantly, also, but she felt a gratitude uncommon in those afflicted in this way. Her suicide was of the heroic kind; she expressed the determination not to drag others through it once more.

The devotion and gratitude are part of a larger, more courteous and loyal time. That is the appeal of Bloomsbury, yes, that and the economy of scholarship. What a relief it is to have a period that has passed into cultural history, but only yesterday, within our lifetime. It is all contemporary and at the same moment also *historical.* Seize the day. It will not last long. No sooner have we taken in Lytton Strachey's homosexuality than *Eminent Victorians* has gathered too much dust.

Virginia Woolf was a feminist. She thought and wrote seriously not only about being a woman but about the defaults and defects of the world made by men. Some of her friends found her insistencies about all this a little sharp and tedious; Forster called her feminism "old-fashioned" and felt, writing in the forties, that it was also unnecessary, since "By the 1930s she had much less to complain of, and seems to keep on grumbling from habit." He goes on from there to the pondering of the ways in which Virginia Woolf was not only a woman but also "a lady." It is with this aspect of her life, the social one, that the English memorialists are, to use a strange American locution picked up from psychiatry, "most comfortable." With us, since our country is not rich in persons even fleetingly acquainted with Virginia Woolf or Bloomsbury, the new phrase is "androgynous vision."*

"Androgyny" is a way of bringing into line the excessive, almost smothering "femininity" of the fiction of a feminist like Virginia Woolf. In her novels there is no work truly understood except that of painting and writing. Men are in politics or law but we see them at a luncheon party and later at an evening party, and both the settings are the feminine domination of the scene, are remarkable for the way in which the men and their work are absorbed, contained, almost erased by the powers of the domestic and the social. There is no novelist whose surfaces are as beautiful as Virginia Woolf's. A mist of loveliness covers everything, even sorrow and regret. The birds sing (" 'how those birds sing!' said Mrs. Swithin, at a venture"), Big Ben tolls, life is a sort of tragic pageant, the Bœuf en Daube browns in the kitchen. The inner life of feeling, the shifting, never recovered, never com-

*Three recent works using this idea and all of special interest on Virginia Woolf: *Toward a Recognition of Androgyny,* by Carolyn G. Heilbrun; *Feminism and Art: A Study of Virginia Woolf,* by Herbert Marder; *Virginia Woolf and the Androgynous Vision,* by Nancy Bazin.

pletely to be known flow of existence—this was the aim toward which she had directed her genius.

"The complexity of things becomes more close," said Bernard, "here at college. . . . Every hour something new is unburied in the great bran pie. What am I? I ask. This? No, I am that. Especially now, when I have left a room, and people talking, and the stone flags ring out with my solitary footsteps, and I behold the moon rising, sublimely, indifferently, over the ancient chapel—then it becomes clear that I am not one and simple, but complex and many."

The "masculine" knowledge a writer like George Eliot acquired from her youth in Warwickshire is way beyond anything Virginia Woolf could have imagined, and thus she could not have created Lydgate and Rosamond, in whom the destructive power of sex and marriage are perfectly and realistically embodied. The aestheticism of Bloomsbury, the "androgyny" if you will, lies at the root of Virginia Woolf's narrowness. It imprisons her in femininity, as a writer at least, instead of acting as a way of bringing the masculine and feminine into a whole. But, of course, the "prison" of words and feelings, the drift and color of things, the losses, the flow of time—these were seized by her as a goal, a pattern, a belief. She is a theorist of fiction, like Nathalie Sarraute, even if they come out at the far ends of Idea. (Perhaps there is something feminist in this, a way of testing and confronting the very structure of the novel itself.)

There was a great mind working in Virginia Woolf's novels. Words, images, scenes, are always perfectly there in her works, but only a great conception could have made history out of the pageant on the lawn in *Between the Acts*. This novel and *The Waste Land* are the most powerful literary images we have of the movement of life and cultures, the dying of the past in the dying of a day, the shift from one order to another in an overheard conversation.

AMATEURS

Dorothy Wordsworth

DOROTHY WORDSWORTH and Jane Carlyle do not present clear possibilities for comparison, but it is not out of order to think of them as products of their place in life—side by side with two of the greatest men of nineteenth-century England. The two women seem to have their being and to have their "work"—if that is the proper word for the journals and letters by which they are known—from the dramatic propinquity of William Wordsworth and Thomas Carlyle. Were they happy or unhappy? Was it enough: the letters, the gatherings at Cheyne Row, the visitors to Grasmere, the household anecdotes, and the walking tours recorded? A sort of insatiability seems to infect our feelings when we look back on women, particularly on those who are highly interesting and yet whose effort at self-definition through works is fitful, casual, that of an amateur. We are inclined to think they could have done more, that we can make retroactive demands upon them for a greater degree of independence and authenticity.

Dorothy Wordsworth is awkward and almost foolishly grand in her love and respect for and utter concentration upon her brother; she lived his life to the full. A dedication like that is an extraordinary circumstance for the one who feels it and for the one who is the object of it; it is especially

touching and moving about the posssibilities of human relationships when the two have large regions of equality. It is
rare and we can only be relieved that Wordsworth understood and valued the intensity of it, did not take his responsibility to it lightly or try to hurt his sister so that his own
vanity might be freed of all obligation. (George Lewes, one
of the most lovable and brilliant men of his day, gave the
same kind of love to George Eliot and to the creation and
sustaining of her genius. A genuine dedication has a proper
object and grows out of a deep sense of shared values. It is
not usual because the arts, more than any other activity,
create around them—at home, with those closest, in the
world, everywhere—a sense of envy.)

We are no longer allowed such surrenders and absorptions
as the Wordsworth brother and sister lived out. The possibilities for this kind of chaste, intense, ambitious, intellectual passion are completely exhausted. Wordsworth would
hardly be allowed, or wish, to dream of setting up with
Dorothy in a cottage, managing their frugal life, starting out
with her help on his great career. Leslie Stephen has him in
youth mooning about uselessly on free will, right and wrong,
revolution, conscience, and "the mysteries of being." Godwin-
ism, with its carefree notions about family ties, was a temptation until Dorothy persuaded him of what he wished above
all to be persuaded of: that he was a poet, nothing else. "It
meant, in brief, that Wordsworth had by his side a woman
of high enthusiasm and cognate genius, thoroughly devoted
to him and capable of sharing his inspiration. . . . His sister
led him back to nature. . . ."

Wordsworth was not attractive in appearance. Dorothy,
walking behind him, said, "Is it possible—can that be William? How very mean he looks!" No doubt she was not
thinking of her own vision, but painfully imagining the skeptical, loveless eye of a stranger upon the precious person. De

Quincey, discoursing upon the valuable, much-tested Wordsworth legs, says, "But useful as they proved themselves, the
Wordsworthian legs were certainly not ornamental; and it
was really a pity, as I agreed with a lady in thinking, that he
had not another pair for evening dress parties. . . ."

Still, dispiriting as his manner and appearance could be at
times, Wordsworth had a surprising, if somewhat dour, gift
with women. He established difficult, enduring relationships
and kept them going with a pedestrian sort of confidence and
trust. When he was young his affair in France with Annette
Vallon was ended by prudence and a little heartlessness. His
money ran out and he was propelled homeward by the
firmest sense of destiny. He clearly could not, as a young
man, live on in France and he could not support a wife, and
he did not need a foreign one. But he kept in touch with
Annette, he visited her on his tours, he met his illegitimate
daughter. No hard feelings—respect, instead.

He married a tranquil, retiring, maternal woman who had
once to him been "a phantom of delight"—or so we are told.
They had five children. Two died very young. A much-loved
daughter died before the poet. William, his wife Mary, and
Dorothy lived on and on. William was eighty when he died,
Dorothy was eighty-four, Mary Wordsworth lived to be
ninety. It was a thorough achievement: love, years, and poems. He never lacked the absolute devotion of women. His
daughter, Dora, entered the list. There was no reason, even
for the abandoned Annette, to fall entirely out of love with
the nice, preoccupied genius who meant her no harm, whose
pride did not need to inflict pain, plan humiliations. But what
did Dorothy signify to him, what do his words really mean?
And what did Carlyle actually think about his wife? Did he
indeed think about her seriously?

Dorothy and William Wordsworth were almost the same
age. They lived all their long lives together except for a few

journeys she made with a friend. They were in their twenties when they visited the Lake Country and decided to settle there. This was one of those decisions, those plot turns of destiny that we cannot question as if they were ahead of us rather than behind us. True, it was forevermore narrowing, confining, and defining, but the country seemed to represent Dorothy's undeviating inclination even more than William's. Other possibilities had already offered themselves to his mind —the city, the university, living abroad, radical groups. Dorothy's life is overwhelmingly affected by the residence in the country: *he* becomes her occupation, her destiny, and what is left over goes to his family, to the hard work of living in the early 1800s.

Hiking trips, observations, the local people, Coleridge, poems read over and over each night by the fireside—this was the natural landscape of Dorothy Wordsworth's interests and talents. Her mother had died before she was eight, her father when she was twelve. She was sent to her maternal grandmother who didn't much like her, then taken to an aunt, finally adopted by an uncle. From her earliest years her situation was close to the dreaded one we find in novels: she was a female orphan. The dearest things mysteriously vanished from her life. She had only her intelligence, her exacerbated sensibilities, and her brother.

There was always something peculiar about Dorothy Wordsworth; she is spoken of as having "wild lights in her eyes," and is remembered as excitable and intense. There is something about her of a Brontë heroine: a romantic loneliness, a sense of having special powers of little use to the world and from which one tries to extract virtue if not self-esteem. She is said to have received several marriage offers, perhaps even from Hazlitt in one of his manic moods. It is hard to imagine any true sympathy between the austere, trembling Dorothy and the Hazlitt who complained that there were no courtesans in Wordsworth's "Excursion."

The enthusiasm for a quiet country life with her brother and his family perhaps cannot be wholly endorsed by contemporary women critics or by female readers given to skeptical wonderings about arrangements and destinies. Still, for Dorothy Wordsworth it was a kind of conquest; lucky, safe, and interesting. It kept her from the horror of "independence" as this condition presented itself to respectable, sensitive young women without sufficient means. The simple, earnest seclusion she had at the beginning with her brother was threatened by Wordsworth's marriage to Dorothy's friend, Mary Hutchinson. But again this worked and she found with them a ground of support, duty, reverence, she could stand on. What alternatives were there—being a governess? Suitable marriages were almost impossible without money, beauty, or some of the scheming acquisitive nature of the lucky young women in the novels of the period. Perhaps writing could have saved her. She wrote, but it was her brother's writing that truly became her lifelong work.

Her journals were begun early, spurred on by William. It appears that he realized the need of an "occupation" for Dorothy, an anchor for her free-flying emotions and impressions. The first notes made at Alfoxden in 1798 set the pattern for all of her writing. It is a peculiar one, trapped in the very weather of the days, concentrating upon the bare scenic surface, upon the ineffable and more or less impersonal.

Bright sunshine, went out at 3 o'clock. The sea perfectly calm blue, streaked with deeper colour by the clouds, and tongues or points of sand; on our return a gloomy red. The sun goes down. The crescent moon. Jupiter and Venus.

What rivets the attention in this early journal is not the moon or the mild morning air, but a sudden name. "Walked with Coleridge over the hills," or "walked to Stowey with Coleridge." Even in her youth in the lake region, nature is not a sufficient subject for the whole mind. To name it, to paint it with words iys indeed a rare gift. But it is a gift almost dangling in the air. It is the final narrowness of the pictorial, the frustration of the quick microscopic brilliance, unroped by generalization.

In "The Grasmere Journal" a few years later, the brief, jagged portraits of country people begin, but there are also desperate hints of vulnerability. When William goes away, loneliness and panic creep in; the time is ruined by the longing for letters, the need for exhausting walks so that one could sleep. William was utterly necessary to give this isolated life meaning; without him the tranquillity was a burden; alone it was nothing but waiting, filling time. Still, he returned and the three months or so at Grasmere with Coleridge, while William was writing the Preface to the *Lyrical Ballads,* were probably the best of Dorothy Wordsworth's life.

The journals are not so much an ambition as a sort of offering. Dorothy seems almost to be making a collection of sights, storing away moments and memories for *his* poetry. Much of what she wrote down is absolutely small, the merest reminder of the sun giving out its rays one moment and withdrawing them the next. She tried later in life to write some poems of her own and they are not good. She did not understand meter and wasn't, in any case, really happy with formal constructions. Most of all, she lacked generalizing power. When Wordsworth says in "Tintern Abbey" that "Nature never did betray the heart that loved her," he was wrong in every way. For him the wanderings, the hikes, gave a depth of scenery into which he poured meaning, philosophy, morality. For Dorothy they were like moments of love, pure sensation that held the meaning of her life without clearly telling her what that meaning was.

The life of Dorothy and William Wordsworth was, as a historical act, a tremendous, demanding game, played for the highest stakes of art. Empson in *Some Versions of Pastoral* speaks of Wordsworth as "doing poetic fieldwork among country people who addressed him as Sir." Dorothy Wordsworth sank into the heavy domestic work on the place. The children were born, there were illnesses, emergencies, as well as the steady demands. She was up at five every day. "We have also two pigs, bake all our bread at home, and though we do not wash all our clothes, yet we wash part every week and mangle or iron the whole." On one occasion she had reason to utter the universal observation of women at home: "William, of course, never does anything."

She undertook the work because it was right and necessary, and more necessary for her than for anyone else, since in a way she was always earning the very right to share their life. But it all had an end in view. The end was the devastating, exhilarating walks and journeys—and the poems. She was creating by her walking, her feeling for nature, her enthusiasm some part of the poems, collaborating in the very private way of love or the highest kind of friendship. This is the way for gifted, energetic wives of writers to a sort of composition of their own, this peculiar illusion of collaboration. The Countess Tolstoy worried and copied and thought about *his* books with an energy that would have put George Sand to shame. Troyat says about her: "Her greatest source of pleasure, however, was not her husband's embraces (she was never a passionate lover), but the manuscript he gave her to copy. And what a labor of Hercules it was, to decipher this sorcerer's spellbook covered with lines furiously scratched out, corrections colliding with each other. . . . Her beautiful curling script flowed across the pages for hours."

In Dorothy Wordsworth's journals there is very little effort made to leave a historical record of her intense knowledge of Coleridge, Wordsworth, Southey, and others. She has little of that instinct and this is odd, especially for an author of casual, day-to-day pages. She is all décor and peripheral characters. She is making a collection of sunsets, rural joys, sustaining the pastoral mood—that is her security in life. She would not dare to analyze *them,* to think about them in relation to herself. It was safer simply to take relationships for granted and to find conflict and character only in the changing weather and sights.

The journals were not meant for publication and her work was not printed until after her death. Sometimes she was urged to publish by friends—the poet Rogers, for instance— but when she thought of that, panic set in. When she tried to be professional she revised too heavily and spoiled her effects. She speaks of having composed *The Recollections of a Tour Made in Scotland*—it was written down after the journey—for a few friends. But it was really, like everything else, for her brother, created in a collaborating mood.

Many of the admirers of the journals search for lines and words that turn up later in poems, as if in this way to vindicate her power, to ensure the collaborative reality. But this seeks to place her too much *inside* the poems, rather than rightly alongside them. And the correspondences noted by scholars are not very striking:

D. Wordsworth: When we left home the moon immensely large, the sky scattered over with clouds. These soon closed in, contracting the dimensions of the moon without concealing her.

> Coleridge, "Christabel":
> The thin gray cloud is spread on high,
> It covers but not hides the sky.
> The moon is behind, at the full:

She sees the famous "leech-gatherer" of "Resolution and Independence." He is sketched briefly in a few details, and nothing is made of him. He confers no philosophical lessons upon the scene. The search for correspondences is, in any case, a misunderstanding of what she was doing in the journals.

To be with her brother in nature was her role. True, she was also an aunt, a helper, a vital part of a close family, but that was nothing beside the spiritual and creative companionship. William's wife, Mary, had an even, placid, warm nature—her part in the rural scenario was set aside for maternity, wifeliness. With Dorothy, so much more vulnerable, a passive sharing would not have been sufficient. And she was not at all tranquil. Instead she was wild, driven, peculiar. Much later, when she is almost sixty, she goes mad, but she is always a little mad and in nothing more so than in her fanatic devotion to her brother.

The journals were the occupation that filled the time left over from domestic work and nature-seeing—the time after tea, before going to sleep. Her energy was overwhelming, rather hysterical and engulfing, too great. In her writing she is settling up the day, putting away the revenue in the cash register. At every moment she seems conscious of what she has to offer. She offers a sportsmanship without fatigue, an eye like a camera's, a nice absence of skepticism. She kept him at Grasmere, working away, and it was necessary to do so since moves were a threat to her place in life—unless the moves were the journeys she excelled in.

By writing her journal she spoke of her belief in the supreme value of their lives. The mornings, the butterflies, the mists, the stops at lonely cottages, the views, the streams, were magnified and glorified by the amount of work she put into them. She looked, she walked, she climbed; she returned home and with her pen looked and walked and climbed again. This double effort seems to be saying to her brother that what they have chosen is literally inexhaustible. One day might flow into another, one walk tread over the same old ground, but look how different they were, how important it was to have experienced the pale moon last night and the bright one this night.

Wordsworth writes a great poem to her, "Tintern Abbey," and there is the deepest agitation and exhilaration of feelings as he calls out to "My dearest Friend, my dear, dear Friend," and "My dear, dear Sister." But we do not know what he made of her life, whether he questioned himself about it. Neither of them liked self-examination; they were private. They accepted and there was, no matter, all the business of actual life to get through; the sorrows and deaths and the writing.

Wordsworth's writing was the moral, emotional, and domestic center of everything and everyone about him. His poems are often autobiographical in a discrete, measured, and spiritualizing way. He likes to think about his wife and his sister, those women profoundly there, and he tells us only of his great fortune in the beneficent souls who cast their lot with him—or whose lot he was to be. "A Spirit, yet a Woman too!" He is very aware of function, both in the sense of the duties of domestic life, and also in the way the affections *function,* easing a difficult, ambitious, creative life. The poems about his wife and sister have a way, at times, of laying them out in hard blocks of definition:

> A perfect Woman, nobly planned,
> To warn, to comfort, and command.

Wordsworth is timid and reserved, and the ironical in matters of human relations is not his mood; marriage, death, love, are to be pondered, carefully thought about without the vinegar of ambivalence. In other respects he is reckless with his invitations, capitalizations, his exclamation marks of intensity and overwhelming feeling. His poem "To My Sister" is graceful, and yet there is something overwrought in it, not entirely pleasing. A suddenly mild morning in March fills the air with magic, transcendence, meaning. He urges Dorothy to come forth with him "after our morning meal is done," to share the mystical promise of the first break with winter.

> And from the blessed power that rolls
> Above, below, above,
> We'll frame the measure of our souls:
> They shall be tuned to love.

In "The Prelude" and in other poems he is tremblingly grateful, beautifully, purely courteous. Dorothy is the source of his right thinking, a muse, his way to an abundant spiritual direction. Without her, "I too exclusively esteemed *that* love, and sought *that* beauty, which, as Milton sings, hath terror in it." So, through Dorothy there is a soothing down in him of the "rock with torrents raging," a gradual domestication, "a kind of gentler spring." We may wonder and yearn more for the terror than for the gentler spring, but there is passion in Wordsworth's poems to his sister; there is great love and gratitude and closeness. His revelation of her is intense and narrow: she is seen as the aide to his work, one who leads him to the proper material, who helps him to find himself, who is right and propitious for his genius. These are in their way love poems, intellectual and family love ("Child of my parents! Sister of my soul!") and shared life.

How moving it must have been to Dorothy to have this externalization in poetry of her central inspiration on Wordsworth, to share his mind and talent with Coleridge, to be important in the shaping of this large, pressing body of work. She was there, honored, thanked, her qualities, some of them at least, admitted to the world in the grandest, highest language. These poems about their exploration of nature are offered for themselves and as a consolation for the griefs that will be sure to arrive.

If solitude, or fear, or pain, or grief
Should be thy portion, with what healing thoughts
Of tender joy wilt thou remember me,
And these my exhortations!

Nothing quite like this comes to mind in literature. We may feel a grain of smugness or some outsized concentration on self in Wordsworth's poems on Dorothy. At times, in some peculiar way, he seems to be *misleading* her, always insisting on the moon and misty mountain-winds as her freedom and salvation. In the end the congratulations are to himself. He leaves out entirely what we imagine she must have often felt—undefined, attendant, dangerously emotional, stumbling. All of this side of her life is a hole, a vacancy; and yet there is no reason to diminish the grandeur, the reality of what she had. Dorothy was to her brother like one of those infinitely vigilant young, beaming wives of very old great men. (They were near to each other in age, but it was often noted that Wordsworth had never been young and there is no doubt he could suffer easily a lot of care and consideration.) Theirs, too, was a marriage of a kind, and it tells us that in the hidden springs of female feeling, sex and children may be forsworn for the passion kindled in the heart by fame and splendor of achievement. It is only something troubling in Dorothy herself that makes us hang back from the assurance that "all which we behold is full of blessings."

The waspish De Quincey did *see* Dorothy Wordsworth; he looked at her very closely, he thought deeply about her. He did not accept anything as given by natural right. His memorial to her is as moving as her brother's poems, and its tone is utterly different from the sentimentality of later writers, such as E. de Selincourt. The idyllic was a part of her nature, but it was also a strenuous creation she had to sustain, a necessity, masking a spirit assaulted by uncontrollable feelings, an extravagant, dangerous temperament, a fitful

education—a person, above all, living out a precarious dedication.

De Quincey does not hesitate to seek for the inside. He
speaks of her "wild and startling eyes," of their "hurried
motions," and he wonders what it means:

Her manner was warm and even ardent; her sensibility seemed
constitutionally deep; and some subtle fire of impassioned intellect
apparently burned within her, which, being alternately pushed
forward into a conspicuous expression by the irrepressible instincts
of her temperament, and then immediately checked, in obedience
to the decorum of her sex and age, and her maidenly condition,
gave to her whole demeanour, and to her conversation, an air of
embarrassment, and even of self-conflict, that was most distressing
to witness. Even her very utterance and enunciation often suffered
in point of clearness and steadiness, from the agitation of her
excessive organic sensibility. At times, the self-counteraction and
self-baffling of her feelings caused her even to stammer. . . .

We had not, from the poems or the journals, known of the
stammering. Also De Quincey tells us there was something
"unsexual" about her; that she did not cultivate graces. But
she was deeply sympathetic and interested in everything
about her. De Quincey noticed the defects of her education
and he was pained to discover the gaps in her learning. He
found her deeply acquainted with certain obscure authors
and yet "ignorant of great classical works in her mother
tongue." He not only notices these things; he makes the effort
to wonder what they mean to her. His conclusions are sad.
In his eyes, the collaboration, the dependency hadn't altogether been for the best.

I have mentioned the narrow basis on which her literary interests
had been made to rest—the exclusive character of her reading, and
the utter want of pretension, and of all that looks like *bluestocking-
ism,* in the style of her habitual conversation and mode of dealing

with literature. Now, to me it appears upon reflection, that it would have been far better had Miss Wordsworth condescended a little to the ordinary mode of pursuing literature; better for her own happiness if she *had* been a *bluestocking;* or, at least, if she had been in good earnest, a writer for the press, with the pleasant cares and solicitudes of one who has some little ventures, as it were, on that vast ocean.

So in Dorothy Wordsworth we see a rare life of the early nineteenth century, a life lived at the creative center of men like Coleridge and Wordsworth. Her fate was edged with luck inasmuch as she shared this life, but it was also shadowed by suffering, instability. She clung to the blessings of her condition and got with them a large measure of unfulfillments. One of the most striking things about the record she left of her life is her indifference to the character of her "dear companions." She could not, would not analyze. There is more to think about the poets in a paragraph of De Quincey's *Reminiscences* than in all of Dorothy Wordsworth. This failure to inspect character and motive incapacitates her for fiction; her lack of a rhythmical ear, her lack of training, and her withdrawal from the general, the propositional, and from questioning made it impossible for her to turn her love of nature into poetry. In her journals there are brief vignettes, good mimicry of countryfolk, but there are no real people—especially she and William are absent in the deepest sense.

We cannot imagine that she was incapable of thought about character, but very early, after her grief and the deaths, she must have become frightened. Her dependency was so greatly loved and so desperately clung to that she could not risk anything except the description of the scenery in which it was lived.

Jane Carlyle

JANE CARLYLE died suddenly one day, in her carriage. She was sixty-five years old and had been married to Thomas Carlyle for forty years. It seems, as we look back on it, that at the moment of her death the idea was born that she had somehow been the victim of Carlyle's neglect. He thought as much and set out upon a large remorse, something like the "penance" of Dr. Johnson, although without the consolations of religion. The domestic torment the Carlyles endured in their long marriage is of a particular opacity due to the naturalness of so much of it, to its origin in the mere strains of living. The conflicts were not of a remarkable kind and domestic discontent was always complicated by other problems of temperament and by the unnerving immensity of Carlyle's literary undertakings.

They were, first of all, persons who drifted in and out of unhappiness, within the course of a single day. Nothing in their lives was easy, and so at one minute they were weary of the yoke and the next quite pleased with themselves. From their letters we can see an extraordinary closeness that took in all aspects of life, the literary as well as the domestic. A lot of letters went back and forth between them because of their pressing need for communication with each other. Except for a period in middle life their vexations were almost worth the pleasure of the telling of them.

They were very much a union. He is Mr. Carlyle and she is Mrs. Carlyle, entirely. Perhaps is it not quite accurate to say that theirs was *the* Victorian marriage; it was an imaginative confrontation from the beginning to the end. The center of the marriage was Carlyle's lifelong, unremitting agony of literary creation, done at home, every pain and despair and hope underfoot. Her genius, in her letters and in her character, was to turn his gigantism into a sort of domestic comedy, made out of bedbugs, carpets, soundproof rooms, and drunken serving girls. Just as the form and style of Carlyle's works set no limit upon themselves, so she sets limits upon everything. His grandiosities are accomplished in the midst of her minute particulars.

The bare facts of the French Revolution, of the life of Cromwell, and all the others were an exhausting accretion. And the style was also an exhaustion: strange, brilliant, the very words outlandish, outsized, epical. Carlyle had an exalted idea of his mission and of the power of literature. He thought of the writer as "an accident in society," one who "wanders like a wild Ishmaelite, in a world of which he is the spiritual light, either the guidance or the misguidance! Certainly the Art of Writing is the most miraculous of all things man has devised. Odin's *Runes* were the first form of the work of a Hero." The capital letter and the exclamation point are Carlyle's characteristic punctuation. Jane Carlyle's signature is the quotation mark of mimicry. Thus the two natures stand in balance, breathing in the coal dust of London, suffering the insomnias, the dyspeptic cruelties of their porridge and potato diets, the colds and headaches, the wrung nerves of two strong and yet precariously organized persons.

Jane Carlyle's letters, published after her death, are more brilliant, lively, and enduring than all except the best novels of the period. She was so interesting a woman, such a good conversationalist, such an engaging storyteller that everyone was always urging her to write novels. Carlyle himself liked to say she had surrendered her own talents in order to help him to have his great career. Among her friends in London there were a number of women writers. Professional activity was not unthinkable or even especially daring—and she was childless and he was busy as Thor up in his study. Imagining Mrs. Carlyle as a novelist is a natural extension of her letters with their little portraits of ordinary people, their gift with anecdote, their fluent delight in the common events of the day. But she lacks ambition and need—the psychic need for a creation to stand outside herself. One of the most interesting things about Jane Carlyle is the predominance of the social in her character. Not Society in any sense of wordly advancement—it was on the ground of the "new aristocracy" that she later suffered wounds from her husband.

The "social" with Jane Carlyle was her interest in the daily, in her chores and friends—her love of gossip and her anxious housekeeping. She was born to live in London, having the sort of nature that took naturally to the city's complaints of exhaustion, headache, and insomnia. Still, there was a good deal of the Scotch Calvinist in both of the Carlyles, and Scotland itself, their birth and youth there, was very much a part of their character. Jane Carlyle kept from her provincial background a large store of Scottish witticisms and phrases and a feeling for the eccentric and unexpected in ordinary persons. She had something of Dickens's eye for the flow of characters in and out of her house, in the street, and also his ear for their characteristic emblems of speech. Dickens was much impressed with her and said when she died, "None of the writing women come near her at all."

The fact of the Carlyles' marriage to each other is somewhat unusual. Jane Welsh was an only child. Her father had been a doctor and she and her widowed mother were important in the town of Haddington. She was thought to be clever and was used to having her own way. Carlyle's family was poor and strict; his father was cold but somehow impressive and the children in the family turned out well. Carlyle himself was awkward, intense, and always special because of his large intellectual powers and ambitious concentration. His powers of mind were the stone upon which the lines and curves of an extravagant, eccentric nature were cut. A description of him, at the University of Edinburgh, before he met Jane Welsh: "Young Carlyle was distinguished at that time by the same peculiarities that still mark his character —sarcasm, irony, extravagance of sentiment, and a strong tendency to undervalue others, combined, however, with great kindness of heart and great simplicity of manners. His external figure . . . was tall, slender, awkward, not apparently very vigorous . . . His speech copious and bizarre."

Jane Welsh's acceptance of Carlyle seemed to rest upon her clear sense of his intellectual worth. She procrastinated, let him know her serious and most capricious doubts. Her letters at this point are impudent, and she seems to feel the courage of her own eligibility and his much smaller claim to consideration. "I love you, I have told you so a hundred times . . . but I am not *in love* with you; that is to say, my love for you is not a passion which overclouds my judgment and absorbs all my regard for myself and others . . . I conceive it a duty which every one owes to society not to throw up that station into which Providence has assigned him; and having this conviction I could not marry into a station inferior to my own . . . You and I keeping house in Craigenputtock! . . . Nothing but your ignorance of the place saves you from the imputation of insanity for admitting such a thought . . ."

Yet she did accept him and she did go to live in the wilds of Craigenputtock for six years. Carlyle was in no sense established when they married; she gave over immediately to her own conviction his great worth. Jane was not sentimental like Dorothy Wordsworth. From the first she began in her letters and her conversation the amused creation of Carlyle at home. As a writer he was self-created, like Zeus, but the living person, gruff, self-absorbed, driven, intolerant, comes to life mostly from her London letters. But perhaps she never got over the feeling that she had, in choosing Carlyle, undertaken an original adventure for which credit was due her. She, for all her wit, was conscious of playing a great role in the creation of Carlyle. Even she was a sort of collaborator in his sacred mission.

The Carlyles are very contemporary. Perhaps the fact that they were childless gives a sort of provisional, trial-and-error aspect to the arrangements of their lives. They set themselves up in Cheyne Row in a respectable and yet properly bohemian fashion. Things were interesting and suitable, but not at all yearning for grandeur or luxury. After her spoiled youth, her brilliance at study, the high place she held among her acquaintances, *this* is what she came to stand on in a private way: properly, if not rigidly, running the house with one servant and sometimes none; prudence with finances, visits to make an appeal to the Tax Collector ("Where was Mr. Carlyle?" they wanted to know); cleaning, dusting, chasing bedbugs, sewing, supervising redecorations.

She did these things with a nervous, anxious sort of Scotch efficiency that never lost some lingering astonishment that such were actually her duties. The tone of her letters is guarded and her feelings are always masked by the wit and the good breeding and pride that made a direct plea for sympathy impossible; it is not easy to judge the true significance of her personal outbursts. After spending an evening mending Mr. Carlyle's trousers, she writes, "Being an only child I never wished to sew men's trousers—no, never." To these duties her charms, the enjoyment people took in her company, her own *fame* as a special person added much. She was admired, treasured, and had her own group of confidants that included Mazzini and the wild novelist Geraldine Jewsbury. But, with some naturalness and a great deal of inevitability, Carlyle took, as a day-to-day matter, her charms and wit for granted. It was still *his right,* his need to scream when the piano started up in the next house, to live out at home the appalling strains of his labors.

His health and his temper were fearful; her health and her tongue were awful. A typical letter:

Carlyle returned from his travels very bilious and continues very bilious up to this hour. The amount of bile that he does bring home to me, in these cases, is something "awfully grand!" Even through that deteriorating medium he could not but be struck with a "certain admiration" at the immensity of needlework I had accomplished in his absence, in the shape of chair-covers, sofa-covers, window curtains, &c, &c., and all the other manifest improvements into which I had put my whole genius and industry, and so little money as was hardly to be conceived!

In the letters it is all turned into a comedy. Carlyle decided that the exhausting redecoration of the house was not enough, that he needed a work place on the top, a room built on the roof. "Up went the carpets my own hands had nailed down, in rushed the troops of incarnate demons, bricklayers, joiners, whitewashers . . . My husband himself at the sight of the uproar he had raised, was all but wringing his hands and tearing his hair like some German wizard servant who had learned magic enough to make the broomstick carry water for him, but had not the counter spell to stop it." She ends her letter with, "Alas, one can make fun of all this on paper; but in practice it is anything but fun, I can assure you.

There is no help for it, however; a man cannot hold his genius as a sinecure."

It is almost ignoble to inspect these domestic letters with anything except gratitude for the intense, flowing picture they give us of a life, for the brilliance of the social history and the way the house, 5 Cheyne Row, becomes a Victorian treasure, itself a character. The value of Jane Carlyle's letters lies very much in their rendering of the prosaic scenery in which a truly staggering Victorian energy like Carlyle's had its existence. *Frederick the Great* took thirteen years in the writing ("Would Frederick had died when a baby," Jane said.); *Oliver Cromwell* burned up four years. This was the way it went on throughout Carlyle's life. His discipline and gospel of Work had its fearful apotheosis in his own practice. This is altogether different from nailing carpets and shaking out curtains.

Jane Carlyle's letters have something subversive in them; the tone is very far from the reverent modes that came naturally to Dorothy Wordsworth. Both the journals of the poet's sister and the letters of the wife of the great prophet are ways of preserving and discovering self-identity. It is easy to imagine that the steady literary labors going on around the two women made a kind of demand upon them; a supreme value attached to sitting at the desk with a pen rushing over the pages. Both had gifts of an uncommon nature, but the casual, spontaneous form of their writings is itself the ultimate risk. We are not *expected* a hundred and fifty years later to have them in our hands, to read them. It is only by the luckiest chance that they survive, and no doubt many letters were lost. Jane's letters might not have been collected, but *The French Revolution* would certainly have stepped forth; *Recollections of a Tour Made in Scotland* might have perished, while *The Excursion* was not written for obscurity.

Jane Carlyle's letters have very much the character of a

social necessity for her. They are meant to delight, to pre-
serve and pass on her unique way of detailing the happenings
of the day. They are pictures of things and people, imitations,
mimicry, autobiography of a narrow sort. Most of the ones
we have were written to family members and to very close
old friends, usually living in Scotland. The largest number
are to Carlyle himself. There is a sameness to them because
the tone is established early and continued long; it is familiar,
light, personal within limits. It tells of an attempt to live in
the midst of things in London, to manage their feelings for
each other, their uncertain temperaments, their unsteady
nerves, his work—to make of all this a life reasonably plain
and undemanding and yet worthy of their odd and valuable
natures.

One of the things that made life hard for the Carlyles was
that they shared alike so many burdens of body and soul;
their complaints ring out in unison and, of course, there is
no one to answer. Their hypochondria and neurasthenia are
scandalous. Jane had headaches, neuralgia that seldom gave
up its dominance, insomnia raging like a train through the
whole night, indigestions, vomiting, aches and pains of every
kind. Harriet Martineau observed that Mrs. Carlyle always
had eight attacks of influenza each winter; she was frail and
exhausted, pale, and yet could be roused from invalidism by
interesting events. Carlyle had headaches, insomnia, dys-
pepsia, indigestion, melancholy, ill-temper, irritability. They
took an enormous number of pills and purges, and it appears
that Mrs. Carlyle in middle life became addicted to morphine. This seems to have caused some of her vomitings and
faintings. During her most suffering years in the early 1850s
she was deranged with depression, jealousy, suicidal feelings.
He too was scarcely ever free from depression and irritability
and was not able to put any kind of rein on the flow into his
mind of extreme opinions and the flow from his tongue of the

same opinions. During his later years Carlyle exhorted mankind to a sacrificial life of Work and heroic, manly Silence. Mazzini noted that Carlyle's love affair with Silence "was only platonic."

There is very little in Jane's letters about Carlyle's ideas or about the actual matter of his books. And, of course, he is all Idea, caught up in a shifting Heroic and Prophetic tendency that finally engulfs him in the unworthy authoritarianism and depressing angers and superiorities of the *Latter-Day Pamphlets.* He scorns Democracy, suffrage. A visit to a reformed prison brings out a hailstorm of hateful pellets of abuse. "These abject, ape, wolf, ox, imp and other diabolic-animal specimens of humanity, who of the very gods could ever have commanded them by love? A collar round the neck, and a cart-whip flourished over the back; these, in a just and steady human hand, were what the gods would have appointed them . . ." John Stuart Mill broke with Carlyle over the violence of his feelings and recommendations, and this work received a bad press generally.

As Carlyle grew older he became more and more aggressive and ill-natured about his contemporaries. His own reputation suffered from his increasing lack of generosity and openness and his peevish self-importance. Visitors to Cheyne Row left in anger and disappointment. Jane is not known to have differed with his opinions, and Julian Symonds in his biography of Carlyle has a distressing picture of a woman who did not combat his warped inclinations on the intellectual level, but grew rather more privately and emotionally bitter and unhappy and crushing to him over personal matters. "There is a story that, in his [Carlyle's] last years, a group of people were discussing in his presence the silliness and blind adulation by which great men's wives often made their husbands look foolish. 'In that respect,' he said, 'I have been most mercifully spared.' "

Indeed Jane Carlyle does not seem interested in the passionate concern for the nature of society's arrangements and values—the flame that burned so madly in her husband. Her friendship with Mazzini was intense. She gave him a lock of her hair and confided some of her complaints about Carlyle, but she did not take seriously any of his plans and hopes for Italy. She had narrowed her sufferings and disappointments down to some private, nagging unfulfillment.

What was the trouble? It is very difficult to set the thing out with any certainty. The incredible question of Carlyle's impotence has no possibility of ever being laid to rest. Froude, the historian-disciple of Carlyle's and the one to whom was entrusted the printing of Jane's letters and Carlyle's strange remorseful memorial to her, seemed to have liked Carlyle a good deal less than he knew. The man was no sooner gone than Froude moved in on the papers, started the biography, and also dealt Carlyle's reputation so many slashes and lacerations it never recovered. Froude said that "Carlyle ought never to have married." The accusation survives, gathering later fuel from Frank Harris's assertion that a doctor examined Jane in her forties and found her *virgo intacta*. Jane is supposed to have told the story about their wedding night—that when he fumbled, she burst out laughing and he "got out of bed with one scornful word, 'Woman!' and went into the next room; he never came back to my bed again."

Carlyle's nature is so confident and expansive it is hard to believe him somehow blocked and incapacitated in this way. Their letters to each other are filled with exuberant appreciation and with an obsessive dependence on the very presence of the other, a condition not likely to lend itself to forty years of chastity and distance. The thing that brought about the pitiful misery and bitterness of the marriage was a matter of at least a secondary sexual nature—Jane's jealousy and fury over Carlyle's friendship with Lady Ashburton. That this jealousy may not have been sexual did not diminish the profound pain of it. It appears that it was in the end Carlyle's insensitivity to her wishes that drove Jane Carlyle into a debilitating madness of rage and depression, morphine and pill-swallowing.

Lady Ashburton was a powerful, intelligent, rich woman who liked Carlyle much better than she liked Jane. She made a great fuss over him, invited them to her country house, The Grange, and called him "her Prophet." At Lady Ashburton's, Carlyle was the star. He who had been accustomed to protesting social life with the complaint that "No health lies for me in that," or "My Welfare is possible only in solitude," suddenly and surprisingly changed his tune and was ever ready to attend functions, long visits, do any bidding. He had never valued idleness, riches, or relaxation, but now he seemed to find the comfortable luxuries of the town and country houses very much to his liking. Authoritarianism and a regard for privilege were growing on him also, like gray hairs he hardly noticed.

Lady Harriet was six years younger than Jane, rather large and utterly, bewilderingly confident of her own worth. She was moderately unconventional but not scarred by a rash of self-examination or complicated modesties and judgments. After Carlyle's acquaintance with her was established, she began to pursue him, to flatter him, to feel quite an urgent need to include him in her circle and in her activities. Lord Ashburton also accepted Carlyle with a good deal of warmth.

Lady Ashburton was not so greatly charmed by Jane. Jane had been adored at home and was much appreciated in London among writers and friends, but her style and tone were not comfortable for the ladies of the aristocracy. She was too ironical and humorous, too quick to identify with a mocking phrase; and most of all, her wit was a sort of private gem. Its sparkle depended upon everyone's understanding the shape of it, the voice. Lady Ashburton was friendly and correct with Jane but it didn't work. Also the society at the Ashburtons', where Carlyle was soon glowing in the attention he received, was much richer and in every way different from the kind of life and purpose Carlyle had taught Jane to value.

The worst of it was that Carlyle had suddenly turned away from his old notions—the Scotch Calvinist ones that had united them. He no longer felt bound by the dogmas of Work, Duty and Spiritual Strength. He now was on the road leading to the New Aristocracy. Lady Ashburton was a good starting point. When she summoned him he would answer, "Sunday, yes, my Beneficent, it shall be then; the dark man shall again see the daughter of the sun, for a little while; and be illuminated, as if he were not dark."

Between 1846 and Lady Ashburton's death in 1856 the Carlyles' life was distressingly unhappy. Their great marriage, the collaboration of two superior, tortured souls, became a nest of miseries, discontents, frustrations. Jane Carlyle's tolerant irony deserted her. She could not bear Carlyle's indifference to her feelings, his neglect of her wishes. It had been bad enough when his work made him demanding and overwhelming, but to have him take pleasure and find relaxation in company other than hers was unendurable. Still, so extreme is her emotion that one can only feel this particular neglect had come to stand for feelings much greater than the friendly, more or less harmless claims of Lady Ashburton.

It seems that all Jane Carlyle's efforts were dramatically brought into question by Lady Ashburton, by her riches, her arrogance, her birth. All of the carpets, the bedbugs, the papering and hammering, the creation of Cheyne Row to encircle and house Carlyle's needs, had been neither the pure expression of Jane's own nature nor a claim, as it seemed, upon his loyalty. For whom had she labored? Running the house with one somewhat shaky servant had been a triumph; the funny Scotch girls were *her* material, and her stories about them are among the best thing in her letters. But her dealings with them show some of the defects and difficulties of her character. Jane Carlyle needed a great deal of care and concern herself. Her disasters with servants were bravely and humorously endured, but her way with them was a mirror showing her deepest, hidden nature—that of a clever, spoiled, and expectant only child.

When a servant appeared she was imagined to be the vessel of goodness, joy, trust; the poor creature was to give the exalted love, consideration, capability, attention, leisure, and comfort Jane Carlyle secretly felt her nature was entitled to receive. "She is by far the most loveable servant I ever had; a gentle, pretty, sweet-looking creature, with innocent winning ways." This is the way the hope rises at the beginning, time and again, but it soon sinks, and the reality are beasts, drunkards, thieves, with no knowledge of cooking or cleaning. With all of this longing never deserting her, Jane Carlyle could feel that in managing to live, to create their lives, at great pains to herself, she was doing something noble and important. Especially because it was she, never meant for it, who was the origin, the mover of it. She had endured Carlyle's bearishness, his grumbling, his fantastic consuming labors, his refusal of practical affairs. She had never felt very capable at the things she learned to do; they were against the grain.

She had sacrificed something—it was not altogether clear —in vain for Carlyle, and that discovery, if such it was, accounted for her exaggerated frenzy over Lady Ashburton. Some of the needs working on him she was not sufficiently knowledgeable about or sensitive to. (Her old indifference to the matter, while treasuring the producer.) Carlyle felt an increasing and insistent wish to shine and to find unplowed souls to shine upon. His ideas and programs were running out. He was a prophet rather worried about the next prophecy. Also in a sad way his own madness was being transformed into character. He was becoming inseparable from his defects and distortions. The projects he set out upon with Lady Ashburton and her friends were small and, even if worthy, retrograde in the light of the larger issues he was turning away from. His projects needed only money; he did not ask that his new friends remake their lives or redeem society. The London Library, new parks, that sort of thing. Members of the aristocracy should "bestir themselves" to fight off the stabs of the lazy rabble at the door.

Carlyle, morose at home, gladdened in the opulent warmth of Bath House, the Ashburtons' house in the city. But for Jane the visits were trying; they created an unease in her spirits and apparently a lowering sense of being an appendage, *there* but not at all necessary. When she showed her distress that invitations were accepted without her agreement, visits were made by her husband alone, even when she was feeling ill and needed him at home. Carlyle became vexed, insensitive to the depth of her unhappiness, or merely willfully indifferent to it. He would write, "Oh, my Jeannie! My own true Jeannie! Into what courses are we tending?" But he would go to the Ashburtons' in any case and remain for five days. For a time he and Lady Ashburton corresponded in secret because of the hysterical frenzy of feeling into which Mrs. Carlyle had somehow thrown herself.

It all seems negligible, out of proportion, one of those trivial points upon which marital rages ponderously come to rest. Still, the angers and quarrels darkened their lives. The sadness is that, even with a clever and uniquely attractive woman like Jane Carlyle, a conviction of having sacrificed only to be undervalued drove her to despair and pulled Carlyle along with her.

At this point she began to keep a melancholy little journal. It is bitter, freely complaining about just those indignities the letters approached with a guarded amusement. There is a measure of vindictiveness in the entries, some eye toward revenge or perhaps only toward the instruction of Carlyle in her true feelings. "That eternal Bath House. I wonder how many thousand miles Mr. C. has walked between here and there, putting it all together; setting up always another milestone and anchor betwixt him and me . . . When I first noticed that heavy yellow house . . . how far was I from dreaming that through years and years I should carry every stone's weight of it on my heart."

Mrs. Carlyle's sudden death plunged her husband into a deep grief. He lived on and on, for sixteen years, always melancholy, lonely, and preoccupied with his lost love and her rare qualities. He saw her journal of the Ashburton years. (Lady Ashburton died in 1856, ten years before Jane. The acute and pointed misery abated, but the general bitterness remained, by now hardened with illness, depression, and the thickening of angry feelings on both sides.) He read over Jane's letters. Remorse struck Carlyle—a strange, repeating, beating, insisting remorse. He treasured the brilliant letters and saw the delight in them and also the undercurrent of breathless effort she had made to create their lives.

His idea seemed to be that she had misunderstood the Lady Ashburton business. "Oh, if I could but see her for five minutes to assure her that I had really cared for her throughout all that! But she never knew it, she never knew it." He collected and edited her letters and gave them at his death to Froude for publication; and he wrote his odd, almost senile, remorseful memorial to her in *Reminiscences.*

He sat down to write, and all the bafflements of Jane Carlyle's place in the nature of things immediately and urgently confronted him. It was not the outlines of her life—that he knew or thought he knew from their long marriage. No, it was much deeper, more puzzling, more to the point. When he started the composition it was not as a family treasure, a book of memory; instead it was to be a real book. What, then, was she that might have a claim on the world's attention by way of print, a sort of biography? Even he could not feel it was as his wife alone that she had her eminence; nor could it be for her highly original and pleasing personal qualities. On the other hand, she was certainly not Schiller, nor even his friend—the preacher Edward Irving or the theologian John Sterling—about both of whom he wrote.

In the end the riddle is never solved and the work is both public and private. It is an ode to a lost love and a curiously, traditionally organized presentation of a life. The beginning strikes a classical note, mixed with worry and compositional confusion about his intentions. "In the ancient country town of Haddington, July 14, 1801, there was born to a lately wedded pair, not natives of the place but already reckoned among the best class of people there, a little daughter whom they named Jane Baillie Welsh, and whose subsequent and final name (her own common signature for many years), was *Jane Welsh Carlyle,* and now stands, now that she is mine in death only, on her and her father's tombstone in the Abbey Kirk of that town."

The work is filled with guilty hyperbole, yet he takes on his guilt so openly, with such a manly fullness that we see it is one of those guilts happily assumed as a gratification to the ego. Still, he must decide what Jane was, what she had given up to be his alone, and he is soon placing her in his thoughts above George Eliot and George Sand in creative powers. With this exaggeration and lack of precision, the excellence of the letters fades. They have not been defined, thought about, carefully placed.

When Jane Carlyle was cleaning and sweeping and keeping the accounts within discreet limits she certainly did not set a price upon her actions. But, of course, there was a hidden price. It was that in exchange for her work, her dedication, her special if somewhat satirical charms, Carlyle would, as an instance, not go out to Lady Ashburton when she would rather he stayed at home. This is the unspoken contract of a wife and her works. In the long run wives are to be paid in a peculiar coin—consideration for their feelings. And it usually turns out this is an enormous, unthinkable inflation few men will remit, or if they will, only with a sense of being overcharged.

It is sad to think of Jane Carlyle's last years. Neurasthenia accounted for a lot of her torments in the middle of the night. But she has such gaiety and reasonableness that we are scarcely prepared for the devastation that swept over her as a result of feeling undervalued, put-upon, refused the consolations of a grateful husband. Once when she told Carlyle that she had, at a certain moment, thought of leaving him, he replied, "I don't know that I would have missed you. I was very busy just then with Cromwell." The raging productivity of the Victorians shattered nerves and punctured stomachs, but it was a thing noble, glorious, awesome in itself.

Jane Carlyle's subversive irony and her ambivalance make her the most interesting of the wives we know about in this period. It is very risky to think of her as a failed novelist or as a "sacrificed" writer in some other form. All we can look for are the openings she—and Dorothy Wordsworth, also— came upon, the little alleys for self-display, the routes found that are really a way of dominating the emotional material of daily life. The chanciness of it all, the modesty, the intermittent aspect of the production—there is pathos in that. In the end what strikes one as the greatest personal loss of these private writing careers is that the work could not truly build for the women a bulwark against the sufferings of neglect and the humiliations of lovelessness. The Victorian men, perverse as many of them are, were spared these pinches of inadequacy, faltering confidence, and fears of uselessness.

SEDUCTION
AND BETRAYAL

SEDUCTION may be baneful, even tragic, but the seducer at his work is essentially comic. It is a question whether there is such a thing as seduction when the affections play a part; and yet this is a murky matter because of the way affections, even those of tenderness and concern, have a tendency to diminish and augment, to transform themselves under the influence of experience, satisfaction, or disappointment. The seducer as a type, or as an archetype, hardly touches upon any of our deep feelings unless there is some exaggeration in him, something complicated and tangled and mysteriously compelling about a nature that has come to define itself through the mere fact of sex. For the most part the word "seduction" indicates effort of a persevering, thoughtful sort. When it is successful we naturally look about for a lack of resolution and resistance in the object; guile and insistence are clever at uncovering pockets of complicity. A seduction is the very opposite of the abrupt, which is, of course, rape.

The most interesting seducers are actually rapists; for instance, Don Giovanni and Lovelace. Their whole character is trapped in the moil of domination and they drudge on, never satisfied, never resting, mythically hungry. The fact that the two characters mentioned are gentlemen gives a stinging complication to their obsessions. Ritual comes naturally to them and birth bestows rights and blurs cruelties. What we may feel is a misplaced elaboration of desire in a gentleman would be in a man of less imagination and of inferior social and personal decoration simply coarse or criminal. In the common man, excessive demand for sex is repulsive. Gentlemen merely run the risk of being ridiculous. To have in Ispagna alone, *mille e tre,* is a most exhausting dedication, and also quite funny.

The danger of ridicule must, in literature, be circumvented if the man is to retain force, magnetism, spirit. (Dignity is scarcely at stake, since it is the mark of a gentleman to look upon dignity as a quality given and once given the last to crumble.) When the Don in Mozart's opera is found in the first scene dragging Donna Anna about, rushing into her bedroom like a burglar, we know that he is a complete fool. ("How can I believe a nobleman guilty of such a crime?" Don Ottavio, another fool, asks.) It is only when the Don murders Donna Anna's father, the Commendatore, that he is redeemed as a character, a creation. He who was a fool has suddenly become sinister, evil, damned; the attention immediately shifts from the victim, the assaulted, sobbing woman, back to the great violator himself. The Don still does not have motive and we cannot understand his raging pursuits, yet we see how complete is his will, his defiance, how devastating his empty energy. The Don will ultimately have, in the opera, a cruel, useless courage in living out his nature to its very end.

In the waste of sensuality, boredom, compulsion, the Don never shows love or pity for the women. That we soon accept, aesthetically, as the frame of the plot of his existence; we are then free to go the next step with him. We accept that he is saved from being a fop by his equal lack of pity for himself. There is nothing self-protective in the Don. If he had called upon the favors of some higher nobility to intercede for him, he would be contemptible in every part of his nature. As it is, he is awful, trapped in his own being. His "extensive sentiments" and his *"tutte quante"* are a malignant growth which he, either by the charms of his character or the weakness of women, wishes to present as a caprice, a temperament, a disposition perfected by a fantast.

Donna Elvira's fascination with the Don makes her a more interesting person than Donna Anna, who is, after the murder and perhaps before, only interested in her father, a totemic figure well-dressed in stone. We do not know whether to call Donna Elvira's attraction under the name of love; perhaps, yes. She herself gives hints of some liking for exorbitance, and her love is scarcely put to the test of endurance because the Don gives her such a short tenure as his betrothed—three days in Burgos.

It is a lack in the Don that he doesn't understand the way Donna Elvira's passion for him makes him a more seductive and profound lover because she is interesting and complicated herself. It does not occur to him that she is an ornament his tawdry soul can well use. Instead he runs around in the shadows of her infatuation, inanely whispering, *"poverina, poverina."* But nothing indeed prepares us for his inexplicably ferocious jest in falsely reawakening Elvira's love only to pass his cloak to his lowly servant, Leporello, and command him to make love to her. The Don sinks here into the depths of coarse, personal dramaturgy. His invention has run out, his labors have exhausted his plotting imagination—and his own delight in the unworthy caper almost destroys him as a character. He would have returned to his condition of fool, if it were not that he is saved again by the indestructible romantic concentration of Donna Elvira. She is soon again pitying him, and by this eternal flaming of hers the Don is rescued from inane buffoonery and restored once more to his interestingly sinister shape.

The *illicit,* as R. P. Blackmur writes in his extraordinary essay on *Madame Bovary,* and its identification with the romantic, the beautiful, and the interesting, lies at the very center of the dramatic action in the novel form. "The more lawful the society, as we say the more *bourgeois* the society, the more universal is the temptation to the illicit *per se,* and the stronger the impulse to identify it if not with life itself at least with the beauty of life." For us now, the illicit has become a psychological rather than a moral drama. We ask ourselves how the delinquent ones *feel* about their seductions, adulteries, betrayals, and it is by the quality of their feelings that our moral judgments are formed. If they suffer and grieve and regret, they can be forgiven and even supported. If they boast or fall into an inner carelessness, what they are doing or have done can seem to be *wrong.* Love, even of the briefest span, is a powerful detergent, but "destructiveness" is a moral stain. In novelistic relations, where the pain inflicted is only upon the feelings of another person, everything is blurred. It is hard to know when rights have been exceeded or when obligations are adamantine.

In *The Scarlet Letter,* has Hester Prynne been *betrayed* by the Reverend Dimmesdale? If the matter lies only inside her own feelings, perhaps we would have to say that she is beyond betrayal. Betrayal is not what she herself feels, not the way her experience shapes itself in her mind and feelings. Love, the birth of Pearl, her illegitimate child, her prison term for adultery, her sentence to wear the letter A on her breast, the insufficient courage of her lover, Dimmesdale— what provocation, what abandonment. And yet these visitations, these punishments, are embraced by Hester like fate. They are the revelations out of which prophecy is made, and so they come to her, not as depressing clouds of consequence, but as opportunities for self-knowledge, for a strange and striking *stardom.*

Dimmesdale, on the other hand, is stunned by the illicit. It corrupts the air around him; he cannot breathe because of his sin. Thinness, pallor, trembling, wasting, heartsickness: such are the words that define his state. He feels his transgression more vividly than anything else in his life. He takes society's attitude toward his adultery with Hester and, thus outcast in his own being, he becomes the betrayed person, almost the *betrayed woman.* D. H. Lawrence's idea that the "greatest triumph an American woman can have is the triumph of seducing a man, especially if he is pure" is a Lawrence paradox arising out of his suspicious dislike of Hester Prynne. It is not true that she seduced Dimmesdale, but it is true in some deep sense that the sexes are reversed in the peculiar terms of his suffering, his sinking under it, the atmosphere around him of guilt, desperation, self-torture, and lonely remorse. The weak and the strong are clearly not where we would expect them to be. Moral courage is the dominating force in Hester Prynne, just as fearfulness, neurasthenic self-abasement are the fate of Dimmesdale.

Still, it would be outside history and a psychological falsification for us to look contemptuously upon poor Dimmesdale. He is occupied with God, truly; he has his mission on earth as a clergyman. His pastorate is serious, his integration in Puritan society is passionate. He is a man in time, living under the dispensation of his moment and his region, Boston, 1642. We cannot condemn his religious scruples, his Puritan dogmatism. We can understand his not wishing to remove himself, by the confession of adultery, from the possibility of bringing light and goodness to his world. It is actually Hester Prynne who is outside history. Her indifference to adultery, her staying on in Boston with her illegitimate daughter, Pearl, her defiance, the striking skepticism of her mind, the moral distance she sets between herself and the hysterias of the time—these qualities are the cause for wonder.

The heroine whose fate is defined by adulterous love is a central and enduring theme in fiction. Love and power are the landscape in which imagined destiny is lived. Power as a consequence of conventional love is suitable for comedies and for the intense dramas of the well-to-do classes and their daughters. Love destroys power in the great tragic heroines, in Greek drama, in Anna Karenina, in Cleopatra. It is infinitely more complicated and mixed in the bourgeois novel. What is asked of the heroine is not always a grand passion, but a sense of reality, a curious sort of independence and honor, an acceptance of consequence that puts courage to the most searing test.

In the novel, when the heroine's history turns about a sexual betrayal, it matters whether she is the central figure in the plot or a somewhat less powerfully and less fully considered "victim" on the periphery. If she is the central figure, psychological structure seems to demand a sort of purity and innocence. Not physical innocence, but a lack of mean calculations, of vindictiveness, of self-abasing weakness. Sexual transgression loses its overwhelming character as a wrong or as a mistake when the persons have virtues of a compelling sort, or spiritual goodness, or the grandeur of endurance. The inner life of the woman matters, what she feels and has felt, the degree of her understanding of the brutal cycles of life.

The problem of creating sympathy for the woman whose destiny must run the narrow road laid out after a disastrous surrender or seduction loomed larger in the minds of authors than it needed to loom. Fiction and drama have always been drawn magnetically to this plot, to this beginning of fated complication, and the situation inevitably partakes of the universal. The experience is common—richly, painfully known, easily imagined and felt. Lust—and then, for the women, stoicism. This is the highest choice. Yet, to be a heroine, to occupy the center of the stage as a sort of incarnation of love or sexual consequence, definite enrichments, heights, intricate particularities must set the woman apart. Her fall or her fate can only be truly serious if a natural or circumstantial refinement exists.

Again Hester Prynne is odd and we wonder how Hawthorne actually looked upon her indifference to society, her radical challenge, her sexual—what to call it?—valor. Of course, Hester is not very greatly under the spell of sensuality. Instead, she is an ideologue, making by way of her adulterous isolation a stand against Puritanism. In many respects, the characters in *The Scarlet Letter* are not characters at all, but large, fantastically painted playing cards. Symbolic action is Hester's role.

Prison, where the novel starts, is a natural school for radicals, especially for those of a theatrical disposition. And Hester Prynne is very much of that sort, a dramatic, theatrical radical. Another radical moralist of the time, Anne Hutchinson, is mentioned early in the book—a woman, banished, rejected, defiant. The two are united in their public characters: Anne Hutchinson begins where Hester ends, working on the minds of troubled women, nursing the sick. And indeed what is Hester's strength except a "covenant of Grace," and a "peculiar indwelling of the Holy Ghost" of the kind Anne Hutchinson laid claim to: both make the claim of personal experience above the social or doctrinal. "What we did had a consecration of its own," Hester says.

Hester is beautiful, dark-haired, dignified, a morally complicated woman who gradually takes on a "marble coldness." She seems dramatically uninterested in religion, just as she is strikingly free in her mind about adultery. "She assumed a freedom of speculation, then common enough on the other side of the Atlantic, but which our forefathers had they known it would have held a deadlier crime than that stigmatized by the scarlet letter." The essential decision of Hester's is "I will not speak," she will not implicate Dimmesdale. She refuses any of the self-saving possibilities—but why? Her "open ignominy" has a life of its own, growing out of the peculiar strength of *the heroine* as a general literary conception. Hester, actually, is in the classical mode: she has a fate rather than a character.

Henry James: "In spite of the relation between Hester Prynne and Arthur Dimmesdale no story of love was surely ever less of a 'love-story.' To Hawthorne's imagination the fact that these two persons had loved each other too well was of an interest comparatively vulgar; what appealed to him was the idea of their moral situation in the long years that were to follow." *The Scarlet Letter* is a drama of sin rather than of love. To Hester the idea that adultery is a crime is scarcely considered; she does not seem prepared to make a stand for "love" or for the purity of her feelings. She is not an apostle for sex. She is a "wild Indian" and, as Hawthorne says, with no reverence left for clerics, judges, gallows, fireside, or the church. It is not against her punishment that she flings herself—"the tendency of her fate and her fortune had been to set her free." She is a natural outcast of the superior sort: serious, somewhat vain of her dignified, sly endurance, attached to the symbolic and emblematic in the usual way of a radical wanting to signify ideas in an outward, concentrated way as he walks among the mass. It is true, as Lawrence says in fury, that she wears her damned A like a duchess's coronet. Everything about her is marvelously dramatic and challenging.

Of course, Hester cannot take the wickedness of adultery seriously because it has brought her little Pearl. Pearl is serious, living is serious, and from the natural pessimism of women with their "imprisonment" in consequence she draws a natural reprieve from the kind of moral lingering in the past that afflicts Dimmesdale. Pearl, her future, the far-flung, unknown life stretching out ahead of the sin: these mean nothing to Dimmesdale. He lingers back, preoccupied with the dead action, the fascination of transgression, the fearful power of it. He is truly in a state of lunacy, as Hester sees when they meet in the forest among the Indians.

Little Pearl, with her "hard, metallic lustre," is a true child of the Puritan inclination to worry the wound. She has no morals at all. She has very early leaped onto another level of possibility and will live it through without remorse or fear-fulness. She becomes the glowing American girl abroad, sending home letters "with armorial seals upon them, though of bearings unknown to English heraldry." Out of this tale of repression and sorrow, of social isolation, spiritual tor-ment, and historical hypocrisy, Hawthorne created two women with fanatical stamina, with an independence of mind and action that went beyond anything the world could rightly have asked of them in their time—or later. Mrs. Hawthorne said, when the book was read aloud to her, that she liked it but it gave her a headache.

Where does the strength come from? First of all it comes from the minds (the observations?) of men, since the novels were written by men and those by women draw largely upon the weight of these powerful conceptions and balance of relations. Women, wronged in one way or another, are given the overwhelming beauty of endurance, the capacity for high or lowly suffering, for violent feeling absorbed, finally tran-quilized, for the radiance of humility, for silence, secrecy, impressive acceptance. Heroines are, then, heroic; but the heroism may turn into an accusation and is in some way feared as the strength of the weak.

The Wife of Bath, coarse, brilliant, greedy, and lecherous as any man, tells a tale of infinite psychological resonance. A young knight who is to be banished from the court for rape is saved by the intervention of the queen and her ladies. He is to regain his place in life by setting out upon a perilous journey to find the answer to the question: What is it women most desire? After the usual torments and trials, the winning answer is discovered: Women desire to have mastery over their husbands.

Novelists are often rather hard on those seduced and betrayed girls who are bereft of heroic quality. Without a transcendent purity of some degree to free them from rebuke and condescension, the girls choke in a tangle of weakness, sensuality, vanity, illusion, irresolution. Hetty Sorrel, in *Adam Bede,* is beautiful, ignorant, fond of clothes; she prefers handsome romantic men to good, kind ones. She dreams in the most provincial way of alliances far beyond her possibility as a poor farmer's niece. George Eliot lays the hand of doom on Hetty for her obtuse hope, her trembling eyelashes, her rushing surrender. She hasn't the quality to be tragic. Instead she is something smaller and lesser—she is miserable. But miserable in the most extreme way, because she is profoundly betrayed by her beauty, by the shallow and easy conscience of her lover, Arthur Donnithorne. Hetty becomes pregnant and sets out across the fields and roads to look for her absent lover; everything about her condition is marked by pain, confusion, helplessness. Love and abandonment have made her as deeply, hideously suffering as some starving, wounded animal. Her child is born and she kills it and is tried for murder.

One of the most brilliant moments in this book comes when we are allowed to enter the seducer's thoughts at just the moment when Hetty—far away—is being doomed. Arthur Donnithorne is daydreaming in his light-hearted, pleasantly self-loving way. He misses Hetty somewhat and yet he feels quite happy imagining that this girl, who has in life just been sentenced to death, must be what his will has ordained for her—agreeably settling down into her proper sphere with her appropriate husband, Adam Bede. Thank heaven it had turned out so well! he thinks.

George Eliot says about Hetty, "Hers was a luxurious and vain nature, not a passionate one." Hetty is susceptible and somewhat shallow. In fiction it is susceptibility that prompts the greatest anguish of betrayal. Women of a more complex character cannot be destroyed in the manner of Hetty Sorrel. Her beseeching glances are the key to an intolerable vulnerability, a lack of spiritual depth. Hetty is soon, as a consequence of seduction, utterly, pitifully desperate. There is everything moving in her bewildered flight to look for her lover, but it is moving in the way of a trapped creature. She has not learned much about herself or human nature; she knows only that she is desperate, miserable.

The author is ambivalent. She doesn't quite respect Hetty, and sympathy is mixed with the thread of exasperation. Hetty has been betrayed, and yet how hard it is to keep from blaming her just a little for her own hell. Sensuality is a burden and sometimes it is touching, but it is not grand, not heroic. Those who suffer from a mere consequence of love, pregnancy, are implicated in their own fall. The consequence is mechanical, universal, repetitive; it will not alone make a tragic heroine or a heroine of any kind. Secret sympathy for the man is everywhere in literature when the mere fact of this sexual cause and effect is the origin of the woman's appalling suffering. If she can be betrayed she is betrayable; we would not expect otherwise of him, the seducer. To accept consequence would ruin his life, be outside his plan, class, history —whatever his own plot may be.

Is it really expected that Arthur Donnithorne, a well-born young man of the gentry class, would marry Hetty, a penniless, beautiful, ignorant young farm girl? No. A reader coming forth with that simple solution would be drastically outside the spirit of the period and of the novel as it was written. Nothing appeared to be less simple than these matters of class in marriage. Fear of misalliances, complications of inheritance, played a grotesque role in the lives of the young, causing respectable girls to live under the shadow of chaperones whose dark ignorance and conventionality were like a withdrawing of the sun. The most elaborate manners, problems of introductions, of walks, of meetings, of parental tyranny, forced marriages, interrupted romances, make of the novels of Jane Austen a sort of social hieroglyph.

No, we accept Arthur Donnithorne's drifting away as we assume a harvest at the end of the summer. He himself comes to a pause in his love, a "natural" one that tells him romance is not static and fixed, but moving and changing in a fearful way. He would like to stop before misery falls, as if he were running from a thunderstorm. His way is a tenderly cruel letter, no doubt sharply and truly expressing his feelings as he understands them.

I have spoken truly when I have said that I loved you and I shall never forget our love. . . . I cannot bear to think of my little Hetty shedding tears when I am not there to kiss them away. . . . And I feel it would be a great evil for you if your affections continued to be so fixed on me that you could think of no other man who might be able to make you happier by his love than I ever can. . . . And since I cannot marry you, we must part—we must try not to feel like lovers any more. . . .

For Hetty the letter was "a horrible sensation" and her dull misery sets in. It is too late, for her; she is stabbed by the letter and stabbed by the consequence of "love"—her pregnancy, which Arthur does not know about. Yet she is not great enough for a transfiguration. George Eliot says that the letter "afflicted her pleasure-craving nature with an overpowering pain." In the use of "pleasure-craving" a judgment is made. We are directed to remember Hetty's thoughtless susceptibility, her lack of a proper cynicism, on the one hand, or a saving resignation, a revelation or premonition of danger on the other. But neither a moral nature nor a bright social intelligence instructs Hetty in the practical possibilities of her romance with Arthur Donnithorne.

She is a victim, of what? Her beauty and her love of trinkets, her insufficient analytical powers, her refusal of intuition, her sensuality, her coquetry, her social class and her lover's higher class. She is a victim of errors, impressions, imperfections. She is merely romantic in an ordinary way, and ordinary romance and longing are not "serious" attitudes for one in her position. Her expectations trivialize her feelings and later her pain, loneliness, and panic devastate her judgment so greatly that she covers her baby with leaves and abandons it in the woods. Hetty is pathetic, her fate is awful, we weep for her—but she is not a heroine. She is an instance, an example, a prisoner of cause and effect: flirtation, surrender, pregnancy, misery. This is the plot of existence.

The fact that Hetty Sorrel is only seventeen will not alter the plot or her downward spiral or our withholding from her, in the terms of the novel, the more deeply felt identifications. She suffers, yes, but we knew that was coming. Nothing surprises us about Hetty's misery. Her lack of foreknowledge is a pity, but it is not redeeming. This is the obdurate cycle. Hetty simply hasn't the right sort of nature, none of the heroine's patience or endurance of the conditions of life, none of those crafty, observant hesitations we would wish from the life of realistic country people. Everything is an illusion except her misery. Nor can she turn inward, for there is just a deadness there. She is like Emma Bovary at last trying to pray for relief from pain. Emma calls out to the

Lord in the same words she had used for her lover. "It was to make faith come; but no delights descended from the heavens, and she arose with tired limbs and with a vague feeling of gigantic dupery."

Roberta, in Dreiser's *An American Tragedy,* is condemned to death for her ordinariness, her whining hopelessness, combined, of course, with pregnancy. Clyde Griffiths is scarcely more propitiously organized and endowed for life than Roberta and yet, in him, the vain, pleasure-loving sensuality that unhinges the fortunes of Hetty Sorrel has the character of social movement, economic hope. We can see that he and Roberta might have come together in loneliness and isolation, but we can also see that Clyde suddenly glimpsing the cars, "the gowns," the parties of Lycurgus will almost immediately find Roberta downward, depressing, beseeching, threatening, and therefore intolerable.

Clyde has the susceptibility of his ignorance. He too is in many ways a trusting, yearning *girl;* he wants to put his fate in the hands of women he feels are superior to him, who own things, who live—as he sees it—with assurance and glitter and possibility. Earlier he is "seduced" by the Green-Davidson Hotel in Kansas City. It is like Hetty with her trinkets. "The wraps, furs, and other belongings in which they appeared, or which were often carried by these other boys and himself across the great lobby and into the cars or the dining rooms or the several elevators. And they were always of such gorgeous textures, as Clyde saw them. Such grandeur."

And when Roberta is desperate, when she is most desolating to Clyde's wishes, it is just then that his shallow and passionate need for glamour, his hope for an easy sliding into prosperity, appear as a true possibility, a swooping stroke of luck. Of course, the reader knows more about Clyde than he can know; he is like Hetty—utterly, foolishly without reservations, without a saving reality. A more serious and

thoughtful and genuine young man would have acknowledged the rebuffs, the petty snobbishness and corruption of
the life he longed for. All Clyde can see in his pitifully
longing dreams is that life seems to beckon, when it truly
does not—and that Roberta is death, which she truly is.
"For, as he now recalled, and with an enormous sense of
depression, Roberta was thinking and at this very time, that
soon now, and in the face of all Lycurgus had to offer him
—Sondra—the coming spring and summer—the love and
romance, gaiety, position, power—he was going to give all
that up and go away with and marry her. Sneak away to
some out-of-the-way place! Oh, how horrible! And with a
child at his age!" Later in his reverie, he cries out, "The loss!
The loss!"

The whole drive of the novel is to make us feel Clyde's loss,
even though we know him born to be a loser. Still, Roberta
is a heavy burden. He is young and his dream, if he is allowed
to share in his uncle's prosperity, is to attain a corrupt,
foolish, vain, and empty life. And yet the injustice is that he
has no preparation even for that, no stamina or hardness; he
has nothing except his own idle need for indulgence, fantasy,
the trinkets of existence. What he needs he does not have:
money, support of family, aggression, will. Nevertheless,
Clyde is the center of feeling in the novel. We pity him and
we pity Roberta and always we pity him more. By her death,
Roberta is caught in the ultimate consequence of sex; but the
electric chair for Clyde seems more horrible, a doom of many
causes, the end of all the false promises of life. The deaths
are not for love, but for sex—the annihilation at the end of
the road when things go wrong and responsibility takes its
toll.

For all Clyde's weakness and vanity, his impossible ignorance and unworthy folly, we agree that somehow Roberta
is exacting too great a price. She asks his whole life, paltry

and trashy as the life he wants may be. For her, what would have made it possible for us to accept her totally, not merely to pity her? Where does redemption for Roberta lie? In fortitude, austerity, silence, endurance. These acceptances for lowly girls are the only paths to moral dignity. The novel —deterministic, bourgeois in spirit for all of its questioning of the hard terms of life—always understands that the men must get on. Dimmesdale must preach and save souls; Clyde must get a job with his uncle and go with the crowd he ignobly admires; Arthur Donnithorne must take over his estates. To ask differently of them would violate the laws of social survival, would impose standards of revolutionary skepticism about the nature of all of society's arrangements.

The idea of sexual responsibility for the passions of youth cannot be understood as an ethical one. Clyde is twenty-one when he goes to the death chamber. Even allowing for the convention of outlandish youthfulness in the principal characters in literature we still cannot wish to decide fates because of fornication. Of course, it is not natural passion he is to pay for, but murder. Still, he was trapped by needs of the most ordinary sort, universal needs, universally satisfied without punishment.

Biology is destiny only for girls. Were everyone in the drama of biology more prudent and watchful of the social and financial outlines of his alliances these matters could be arranged, manipulated. But just as the illicit is the trembling attraction of the novel, so is the illicit between persons of different rank, different natures, a variation that stirs our sense of the dramatic instabilities and violations of love. We know that we are near our own time when a novel can concern itself, as *An American Tragedy* does, with two people, Clyde and Roberta, both deprived, stunted, pitiable. In spite of the equity of deprivation, it is Clyde's lack of resignation to a future darkened by Roberta's pregnancy that moves us, keeps our sense of the intolerable blackness of consequence alive. The mind protests for both of them. It is only that Roberta, trapped, miserable, imagines existence would be possible if only Clyde would take care of her, settle in for life. We cannot quite forgive her the simplicity.

The Kreutzer Sonata, by Tolstoy, is a work of great peculiarity. It is not of the first interest imaginatively, and there is a dense, frantic distortion in this pedagogic monologue on sex and the ills of marriage. It is a tract, inchoate, and yet noble, impractical, original. There are moments of dramatic genius: a wracking vision of marriage as jealousy nourished, hatred voluptuously fed, rage taken for breakfast. The whole of a man's sexual life comes under Tolstoy's agitated scrutiny—from the arrogant encounters of youth to the fevered tournaments of conventional unions. Tolstoy sees the line of "immorality" beginning in the young man's first relations with prostitutes and girls toward whom he feels no obligation; from there all of the later life of the sexes is either grossly or subtly poisoned. Life among men and women is a debauch the young are led to accept, even to expect, by custom, example, social convenience.

The actions the nineteenth century gathered together under the name of "debauchery" are never, in fiction, made entirely clear, but it seems very likely that many of them are understood in our time as healthy exertions of vital being. Debauchery, of course, still exists in our minds as a designation of brutal excess and deviation, even if it cannot stand as the name of the experiences of the man in *The Kreutzer Sonata.* "I did not understand," he says, "that debauchery does not consist simply in physical acts . . . real debauchery consists in freedom from the moral bonds toward a woman with whom one enters into carnal relations. . . ."

No doubt it is spiritual vanity and overreaching to hope

to enchain the baffling, exciting, fleeting movements of the senses. Every moment of the present is rushing into its fate as the past. To give the past preeminence, sanctity, supreme right, is insupportable, a mad dislocation in the economy of personal experience. Nevertheless, the past is not a blur of memory, but a forest in which all of the trees are human beings, rooted, breathing, sustaining the ax, or withering. To think of the past as a series of agreements with others that make an everlasting claim on us is unreal, and yet it is one of the most interesting questions ever asked about the subject matter of so much art: youthful love. It is a radical questioning of the way society understands the flow of life, the rules it has made for the human collisions that are, finally, our biographies. It is a question that goes beyond an answer.

Resurrection is a much greater and more moving asking of the same question. The pure situation of this novel contains the essence of the theme of seduction and betrayal. Every balance is classical. A man, a nobleman, falls in love in youth with a serving girl on his aunt's estate. She is lovely and pure; he is generous, kind, better than most young men. The scene of their first coming together is tenderly ardent and promising. It is spiritually coherent, beautiful, merging like a mist with nature. When the night is over, a sweep of sadness causes the young nobleman to ask himself, "What is the meaning of it all? Is it a great joy or a great misfortune that has befallen me?" But then he remembers that everyone does it and he turns over and falls asleep.

Naturally the young man goes away, as he must, since all of his life is before him. It is a life at once free and fixed. Years and experience leave room for the accidental, the free flowing of existence; form and structure draw the prince inevitably into the anxious considerations of a man of his class. Shall he marry the shallow Princess Korchagina, whom he cannot even see without a feeling of impatience and weariness; shall he break off his affair with the wife of a friend; what to do about his estates?

For Maslova, the young girl, his first love, the seduction is a catastrophe. It is not a disillusion that will be washed away by time, but a tragic circumstance from which enormously varied lifelong sufferings begin to follow. She becomes pregnant, is turned out of the house; the child dies, and through poverty, ill-treatment, and despair Maslova finally becomes a prostitute and is accused of murdering an old client. The worst of her sense of abandonment comes when the prince does not even get off the train as it passes through the village some months after their affair, when she is already aware of her condition. Her horror is an intellectual crisis as much as a personal deprivation and pain. God and His laws are a deception. The prince who had treated her so heartlessly was the best person she knew; "all the rest were still worse." It came to her, as the train pulled away, that everyone lived for himself alone and she began to accept an existence encircled by melancholy, redeemed by a willed anesthesia toward the past, enriched only by the communal traditions of prostitution.

The novel's moral judgments lie upon the soul of the prince. Maslova has remained alive somewhere in his consciousness, a dormant germ of remembered feeling and guilt. They meet again when the prince is called to jury duty and Maslova is in the dock, her fate at the end of the trail that began long ago in a beautiful scene, a snowy midnight Mass in the village. The prince is overcome by a violent turmoil that shakes his whole being; he is seized with the wish for a grand restitution, a sacrifice, a determination to share Maslova's degradation and suffering as a prisoner in Siberia. This cannot merely be a flight of fancy. To face the dragon of responsibility would engage his whole life, his estates, his money, his friends, his career. All of the arrangements and assumptions of society went into his seduction and abandonment of the poor orphan on his aunt's estate. His expiation cannot be selective. In the end, Maslova refuses his sacrifice and will not marry him. It is too late for them.

Tolstoy was in his seventies when he wrote *Resurrection.* The indulgences of his youth thus presented themselves to his imagination as moral and social delinquencies, rather than as mere instances of man's inevitable practice. For this reason and despite the marvelous truthfulness of a great deal of the novel, it relies upon the silky transcendences of persons in the grip of a spiritual idea, characters who must go from flaw to virtue under the rule of justice and ethical revelation. However, it is certainly never Maslova's suffering and resignation we question. It is only Prince Nekhlyudov's profound sense of obligation, his heeding the affliction of memory, the bite of the past, that strike one as abstract, programmatic, untrue to life.

The title of the novel is accurate—drastic breaks with the customs ruling men and women are to be understood as a "resurrection," a surpassing. It is, after all, only an ideal, the dream of an old man in love with humility and longing to achieve a personal reformation upon which a reformation of society might begin. The novel was based on an incident that appeared in the press and stirred Tolstoy's thoughts and imagination. In spite of this, it is realistic only in the grand, elevated Russian novel sense, in that landscape where obsession and transfiguring guilt and expiation are real. No subsequent novel decided to gaze so directly into the abyss of sexual responsibility, to turn a limpid, childlike, old-man's eye upon the chaos of youth, to undertake a day of judgment account.

Richardson's *Clarissa* is openly, and at great, fascinating length, about seduction. Naturally, only a person who thought of himself as a moralist could sit down to write volume after volume of consummation threatened and delayed, assault planned and outwitted. Richardson thought, or told himself that he thought, of his brilliant creation as a sort of encyclopedia of male guile and treachery, an elaborate, defensive karate, by which the menaced girls of the eighteenth century could learn to protect their virtue. The detail is intricate, the postponements and escapes are frenzied, the characters extraordinarily well matched in their odd strengths. All of the action is accomplished under the strict baton of sexual suspense.

Clarissa is a disturbing mixture of wit and sentiment, of surface and disguise. A good deal of emotional anxiety accompanies the modern reader along the way here. The novel that caused all of England and Europe to cry—Rousseau yes, but Diderot!—and opened the seams of sensibility and romanticism, as if discovering new minerals in the soul, is harsh, ugly, and grotesque, concerned with a purely sexual conception of virtue and villainy, a conception heavily under our suspicion.

Insolence and courtesy, or at least an elaboration of manner passing for courtesy, are so closely interwoven in the style that they represent an aesthetic exhilaration. The wit, the speed, the expressive, fantastical elegance of the letters that tell, with the wonderful, lost slowness of past times, this violent story are the vehicle for an unmotivated need for sexual humiliation on the part of Lovelace and a need to encounter but avoid the violation on the part of Clarissa.

Clarissa is a bourgeois heroine, the defiant but deeply alert and prudent daughter of rich parents who have not reached the point of trusting the sentiments. (Clarissa's prudence is sexual; otherwise she makes every mistake possible to a clever, bossy, morally vain young girl.) The rich, handsome, brilliant rake Lovelace seeks to marry her, partly to unite her father's money with his own name and lands. Another suitor, whose property is close to that of the Harlowe family, is produced for Clarissa, but she does not love him. He is not lovable and she, asserting the dominance of feeling over calculation, refuses to marry him. She says she would rather remain single, and in many ways this threat appears to be, in fact, a condition Clarissa could have endured with a pleasure equal to fortitude. But the compulsion the stupid family puts her under is so great, the challenge to Lovelace is so sportingly exciting that he abducts her, and the intense, quivering drama of seduction and escape begins. Clarissa's virtue and Lovelace's determination: this is the balance of the longest novel in English.

The fact that the novel is written in letters is of the greatest importance. The depravity of the plot is in that way kept at a distance. And the use of letters modifies the inner life of the characters as we know them. A letter is not a dialogue or even an omniscient exposition. It is a fabric of surfaces, a mask, a form as well suited to affectations as to the affections. The letter is, by its natural shape, self-justifying; it is one's own evidence, deposition, a self-serving testimony. In a letter the writer holds all the cards, controls everything about himself and about those assertions he wishes to make concerning events or the worth of others. For completely self-centered characters, the letter form is a complex and rewarding activity. Both Clarissa and Lovelace are self-centered. They *must* tell their story, must objectify everything, even sexual assault. Reality lives in words.

Lovelace to his friend:

Her chamber door has not yet been opened. I must not expect she will breakfast with me. Nor dine with me, I doubt. A little silly soul, what troubles does she make to herself by her over-niceness! All I have done to her would have been looked upon as *frolic* only, a *romping-bout,* and laughed off by nine parts in ten of the sex accordingly. The more she makes of it, the more painful to herself, as well as to me.

The story moves back and forth in brilliant communications. It comes to a sordid end. Lovelace takes Clarissa to a mean, filthy brothel, finally puts her under the care of two revolting procuresses, has her drugged—and at last rapes her, since she will not have it otherwise. When she recovers, Lovelace wishes to marry her, but Clarissa refuses, wastes away, and dies. He is killed in a duel about the affair.

Lovelace is a monomaniac who seeks life through sex. He is somewhat like the sleepless seducers in Restoration comedy, but on a grander scale. His wildness, his nihilism, his brilliance, his boredom, his sexual pride, are altogether original and exceptional. There is, as in Don Giovanni, an absence of motive and an exorbitance of obsession. His fascination with Clarissa is usually spoken of as "love," and yet his determination is not to win her in marriage, although that is part of the plot, but simply to destroy her virtue. It nags him, exhausts him, bores him—but he will not leave off.

The plot moves on the unconscious curiosity Clarissa feels about Lovelace, her paralysis before the hypnotic appeal of his thoroughly deserved evil reputation. She says early in the book, "I like him better than I ever thought I should like him and, his faults considered, better than I ought to like him." What does she like in him? In every way she would wish the chance to reform him, to exercise her will to power in that fashion. A hopeless, ill-placed wish it is, but she is not easily deflected and is ever eager to find reasons for excusing his villainy. Should there be possible a means of interpreting the most dreadful behavior in Lovelace's favor she will find it, even though she never loses her hard-headed suspicion of him. "You may observe," Dr. Johnson said about Clarissa, "that there is always something she prefers to the truth."

Clarissa seems to entertain more hope for Lovelace than we do; at the same time she has none of our fascination with his mind, his cutting irony, his reckless skepticism. She knows little about all of this because she hasn't read his extraordinary letters—and we have. His driven energy, his interesting ruthlessness do not seem to be the springs of her attraction; she is compelled by his good looks and his bad reputation. It doesn't appear egregiously modern to speak of her hidden curiosity, her complicity in her own humiliation, her lingering about dangerous premises, the interest of the final drugged immobility which is the long delayed condition of her violation. Her dignity afterward is another thing—her saintly suffering, the apotheosis of degradation which truly ennobles her, like a salvation finally achieved. She is going to die and even that is plausible on the practical level in a world of early deaths, pneumonias, tuberculosis, decline.

Clarissa is not seduced, cannot be seduced, fraudulently led into adultery. She can be raped, just as anyone can be. This is the meaning of the violation in the book, that she is literally unseducible and if the man is bent upon consummation he will finally have to knock her out to have his way. Lovelace hates Clarissa's family for their bourgeois lack of excess and their hesitation about aristocratic indulgence. This is one of the reasons he grimly wishes to subdue the daughter. Even more he wishes to destroy Clarissa's will to power through virtue. As a rake, a clever man, he must have known a great deal about the need to dominate in a certain sort of aggressively pure woman. He is himself an independent, spoiled man and Clarissa's degree of overwhelming virtue enrages him and stabs at his sexual pride.

The frustrations imposed by virtue may annoy a man like Lovelace, but the destruction of them will not redeem him. He is redeemed by Clarissa's powerful attraction to him, her absolute need for him, her bewildering inability to withdraw from the game of seduction. There is a fire at the inn where they have taken rooms in the flight from her family. This occasion finds her in her bedroom, frightened, half-dressed, "exposed"—and indeed Lovelace sees the emergency as the opportunity to accomplish his wish. Screams, prayers, pleas, tears finally exhaust him, but not before he has behaved violently, heartlessly. What does Clarissa do? She puts him on a one-week probation.

Her experiences throughout the novel are extremely sordid. The inn and the prostitutes are quite startling in the authenticity of their squalor. "The vile house," Clarissa calls it. She lives in terror of Lovelace—the kind of "terror," domesticated, part of a risky tournament, a wife long married might speak of. "He terrified me with his looks, and with his violent emotions, as he gazed upon me. . . . Never saw I his abominable eyes look as they looked. . . . And yet his behavior was decent, for he snatched my hand two or three times, speaking words of tenderness through his shut teeth." Lovelace speaks of Clarissa as a "poor plotter" and we are bound to admit the accuracy of the observation, as she seeks the net she flees from.

Rage and vanity are Lovelace's traits. Virtue, love of power, and curiosity are the defining marks of Clarissa's nature. The novelist, Richardson, understands cruelty in his own angular, disguised way. It is only a few plunges downward to *Les Liaisons Dangereuses.* The two works are connected by their sexual and social brutality. The industriousness of *Clarissa,* the sense of an indefatigable, brilliant mind (Richardson's) behind it all, gives the work its outrageously fascinating character. But the power of the story lies in sex. Only on the surface is it a game of marriage and family. Clarissa is drugged and raped—this is the end of the line, a resolution. It may be a crime, but it is not exactly a betrayal of her expectations.

The intention of seduction is evident from the first meeting of Clarissa and Lovelace. Attraction, "love," is also at stake. If Clarissa is betrayed, she is betrayed in her determination to reform, and by her fussy capability all turned useless because of the undertow of fascination. Clarissa courts danger and then insists upon her safety. She is a middle-class girl, used to the love of her family, secure enough to defy, run away, and yet call upon the higher sensibilities of personal feeling as her judge. In that way she has none of the vulnerability of Tess, Hetty Sorrel, Jane Eyre, all of them poor and alone. After all, Clarissa lives in a social whirl of correspondents; she greets the morning mail as if it were a row of bodyguards. She replies, at length, in a frenzy, and is, thereby, the least isolated of threatened girls. Words are her protection. Her cries to heaven go out in the next post. Her powers are not perfect, but they reduce the insuperable Lovelace to rape, the most unworthy resource. Are they lovers, or opponents? They have furiously, curiously tested each other and the consummation is death.

Tess is the most perfectly conceived of the modern betrayed heroines. Peasant stoicism and a natural refinement of feeling are especially moving in her because of the hard soil they have grown upon. It is not pride that sustains her, that keeps despair from rotting the character. Pride would rest upon disappointed hopes in the matter of respect and consideration felt to be forthcoming, and it is just the absence of such expectation that distinguishes the afflicted heroine in the novel form. Hester Prynne does not have pride; she has endurance and intellectual principles. Maslova, in *Ressurection,* is supported by her world of the oppressed, accused, imprisoned, and in her earlier years by alcohol and depressed bouts of dissipation. It is part of the magic of Tolstoy's sympathy that allows her to be a drunken prostitute without losing the essential stoical, enduring heroine quality.

Pride is the way of the tragic Greek heroines—not the answer in the more practical, reduced world of the novel. Here the women must deal with betrayal as a fact of life. Through their experiences, the terms and promises of romantic love are brought into question in the deepest way. Sentimentality is false and shallow, and to rely on it is the mark of an inferior vision of life. Trust will not be honored, since it is difficult, in matters of love and sex, for human beings to hold to it. Life will not accommodate.

Hardy saw the necessity of rooting the beauty of Tess's character in plausible superiorities that would set her apart, without pretension, from her world. She comes late of the old noble line of D'Urbervilles and represents an impoverished thinning out of a dead ancient family. (It is interesting that the rest of her family, rather comically inclined to daydreaming and fecklessness, do not partake of any special qualities because of the thin thread of the bloodline.) Her seducer, Alec D'Urberville, does not have as true a claim to the name as Tess, but he is rich and, of course, all of his possibilities, the demands and blemishes of his character, are altered by the inward and outward results of riches.

Tess is also made a high school graduate so that she can be rescued from the benign ignorance of the other farm girls. But she is a farm girl, nevertheless, possessed of an extraordinary naturalness, fineness of nature, with everything rustic and simple and strong that a pure peasant culture could provide. The qualities of her nature, the way she is somewhat set apart, are necessary because she is to receive every blow and, as a heroine, must be worthy of her calamities—sex, love, pregnancy, abandonment, poverty, coarse work, ill luck, and finally execution for murder.

Tess's love affair with Alec D'Urberville is a sort of seduction, at least from the man's point of view. Seduction is his aim, and he works to accomplish it by flattery, pretense, and finally a rude, overwhelming insistence. It is not the usual seduction because Tess never really likes him. She is not swept off her feet by illusion and hope, and yields only with a hesitant acquiescence. It is life that acquiesces, not her nature or soul. She is much too real in her own feelings to put any trust in the intentions of Alec.

And yet it happens that the night with Alec D'Urberville ruins Tess's life, even finally takes her life. It is the beginning of the most painful, devastating series of entanglements and misfortunes. There is a child born after the seduction; she humbly takes the responsibility upon herself. The child dies and does not seem to have had great significance for her, perhaps because of her lack of love for the father. It is not the child that casts such a long shadow but the affair itself, her fall, her acquiescence. Through it she loses her real love, Angel Clare.

Angel is the son of a clergyman, and does not wish to go into the professions. He meets Tess when he comes to learn about farming at the dairy where she works. They fall in love, genuinely, truly. They marry. An unvoiced knowledge of human nature causes Tess to be silent about her earlier affair; hesitation is the measure of her hazy acknowledgment of Angel's limitations, of the narrowness of his break with the pieties of his class. On their wedding night, Angel himself confesses the dissipations of youth, and Tess, in a spirit of reciprocity, trust, and wish to unburden herself, confesses her own affair with Alec. Angel is horrified, leaves her, and goes off to Brazil. Like Dimmesdale he cannot ask fundamental questions about life. Any callousness is possible therefore, and his crushing rejection of Tess is one of the most cruel things in fiction. The dense brutality of it is felt bitterly because of Hardy's genius in revealing how great their love was and the miracle of their passing through the falseness of life to find this great and pure love. The deliberate destruction of miraculous love out of regard for—what? A vanity based on the dimmest flutterings of custom.

Dimmesdale's religion and Angel Clare's double standard are real enough, but it is not easy to give them an equal right to consideration. Religion was the whole of this life and after to Dimmesdale, and his last action is an "Election Day" sermon. For Angel, a skulking vanity and tribal narrowness caused him to abandon Tess. One feels at this point a certain attraction to the abstract in him; he would not have married Tess if he had not had a generalized, formal picture of her as a beautiful, virgin girl of the peasant classes he alone had discovered. The truth of his real love for her is that he suffers almost as much as she from his abandonment and yet he cannot reverse the course of his pedantic decision. The end of the plot is that Tess kills D'Urberville and is executed for it. That is the last act of the drama that began on the night of her seduction.

Hardy sees Tess as a beautiful, warm soul run down by the dogs of fate, in her case the bloodhounds of sex and love, Alec D'Urberville and Angel Clare. Her acceptance, her endurance of the griefs of experience, are of the heroic kind; she meets suffering without losing her capacity for feeling. She is not surprised by loss and rejection and therefore never degraded by it. In Tess's life every adversity has its double. Her misery over the flight of Angel Clare goes hand in hand with a deepening poverty and a deadening solitude. Toward the end of the book her family is actually starving and it is for that reason she takes up with D'Urberville once more. She is defined by her work. The arch of her existence curves as much with work as with love.

Tess's early days on the green dairy farm are idyllic, and the fields and cows coincide with youth and love. In the end she is living in the dismal town of Flintcomb-Ash, working at a threshing machine rented by the day. The farm has become a factory and some critics think *Tess of the D'Urbervilles* is about the death of the English peasantry. The destruction of Tess's love is like some eternal winter, and the scene of her final despair is a bleak and barren epic:

. . . strange birds from behind the North Pole began to arrive silently on the upland of Flintcomb-Ash; gaunt spectral creatures with tragical eyes—eyes which had witnessed scenes of cataclysmal horror in inaccesible polar regions of a magnitude such as no human being had ever conceived, in curdling temperatures that no man could endure . . .

In the end Tess kills D'Urberville because he ruined her life, even if her real ruin came from Angel Clare. Hardy has great pity for Tess and yet he has not made of her a theme but a whole person, one of the most original women in fiction because of her naturalness, which never exceeds the possible. He takes a view of the social forces working upon her in his subtitle, "A Pure Woman Faithfully Presented," and in chapter headings such as "The Woman Pays." She is nevertheless a paradox of the kind that seems to come unbidden into the minds of novelists when they face the plot of sex and its destructive force for women. She has, for all the truth that the Immortals are having their sport with her, for all the malign force of circumstance, suffered in a transcendent stoical way, accepting first her child and then the rejction by Angel Clare as a pattern of social destiny, deeply woven into the cloth of life.

The betrayed heroine, unlike the merely betrayed woman, is never under the illusion that love or sex confers rights upon human beings. She may, of course, begin with the hope, and romance would scarcely be possible otherwise; however, the truth hits her sharply, like vision or revelation when the time comes. Affections are not *things* and persons never can become possessions, matters of ownership. The desolate soul knows this immediately, and only the trivial pretend that it can be otherwise. When love goes wrong the survival of the spirit appears to stand upon endurance, independence, tolerance, solitary grief. These are tremendously moving qualities, and when they are called upon it is usual for the heroine to overshadow the man who is the origin of her torment. She is under the command of necessity, consequence, natural order, and a bending to these commands is the mark of a superior being. Or so it seems in the novel, a form not entirely commensurate with the heedlessness and rages of life.

The men do not really believe in consequence for themselves. Consequence proposes to them a wordly loss and diminishment they will not suffer. They will not marry the barmaid or the farm girl or the unvirginal. They will not confess to adultery when their success or their comfort hangs in the balance. They will not live with the mistakes of youth, or of any other period, if it is not practical to do so. Sex is a completed action, not a strange, fleeting coming together that mortgages the future. For this reason perhaps, the heroic woman had to be created in fiction. "Ah, she will not speak!" Dimmesdale cries out. When they take Tess away to be hanged and to bury her body under a black flag, she has nothing she can say except, "I am ready." Maslova, at the end of her story, turns to Prince Nekhlyudov and says, "Forgive me."

Sex is a universal temptation and activity and a great amnesty will naturally have to attend it throughout life. Scarcely anyone would wish it to define, enclose, imprison a man's being. Society has other things for him to do, being a soldier for instance—a group notoriously indifferent to sexual consequence. Obligation is so often improvident, against thrift. Still, the break with human love remains somewhere inside, and at times, under rain clouds, it aches like an amputation. But it is not *serious*. George Eliot said that she wrote novels out of a belief that a seed brings forth in time a crop of its own kind. How to the point is this metaphor for the plot of the illicit, the plot of love.

Now the old plot is dead, fallen into obsolescence. You cannot seduce anyone when innocence is not a value. Technology annihilates consequence. Heroism hurts and no one easily consents to be under its rule. The heroines in Henry James, rich and in every way luckily endowed by circumstance, are seduced and betrayed by surfaces, misled because life, under certain rules, is a language they haven't the key to. Feeling and desire hang on and thus misfortune (if not tragedy) in the emotional life is always ahead of us, waiting its turn. Stoicism, growing to meet the tyrannical demands of consequence, cannot be without its remaining uses in life and love; but if we read contemporary fiction we learn that improvisation is better, more economical, faster, more promising.

Sex can no longer be the germ, the seed of fiction. Sex is an episode, most properly conveyed in an episodic manner, quickly, often ironically. It is a bursting forth of only one of the cells in the body of the omnipotent "I," the one who hopes by concentration of tone and voice to utter the sound of reality. Process is not implacable; mutation is the expedient of the future, and its exhilaration too.

At the end of *Nana,* the beautiful, harassed courtesan's death mingles with the agitated beginning of the Franco-Prussian War. "*à Berlin! à Berlin! à Berlin!*" we hear outside. In her coffin, fouled by small pox, passion and sensuality are reduced to a "bubbling purulence," a "reddish crust." It is more than that. It is the death of sex as a tragic, exalted theme. As Zola says, "Venus was rotting."